THE SPIRITUAL EXERCISES
MADE IN EVERYDAY LIFE

This book is
No. 8 in Series II: Modern Scholarly Studies
about the Jesuits,
in English Translations

Gilles Cusson, S.J.

THE SPIRITUAL EXERCISES
MADE
IN EVERYDAY LIFE

A Method and a Biblical Interpretation

Translated by
Mary Angela Roduit, R.C.
and
George E. Ganss, S.J.

THE INSTITUTE OF JESUIT SOURCES
St. Louis, 1989

This book is an authorized translation of *Conduis-moi sur le chemin d'éternité*, by Gilles Cusson, S.J., 1973, published by Les Editions Bellarmin, 25 Jarry Ouest, Montréal, P.Q., Canada H2P 1S6.

This is the
First Edition, for the Americas, Western Europe,
Australia, and New Zealand

Note: There is a Second Edition, authorized for
sale only in Asia and Africa, which can be
ordered from *Gujarat Sahitya Prakash,
Anand 388 001, India*

Library of Congress Catalog Card Number: 88-83844
ISBN 0-912422-90-4 clothbound
ISBN 0-912422-91-2 Smyth sewn paperbound

TABLE OF CONTENTS IN SUMMARIZED FORM
(For a detailed table of contents, see page 157)

Editor's Foreword   vii
Author's Introduction   xi
The Text of the Nineteenth Annotation   2
Abbreviations Used in the Footnotes   2

PART I. GENERAL INTRODUCTION

Ch. 1. The History of "Nineteenth Annotation" Retreats   3
Ch. 2. The Method in General   17

PART II: THE EXPERIENCE OF RETREATANTS AND ITS EVOLUTION

Ch. 3. The Viewpoint of Faith Which Puts All Things into a
        Unified Order: The Principle and Foundation   31
Ch. 4. The First Week: Integrating the Problem of Evil into the
        Viewpoint of Faith   41
Ch. 5. The Second Week: The Kingdom and the Deepening of One's
        Spiritual Life   59
Ch. 6. Christ and His Saving Mission: His Infancy and Hidden
        Life as a Prelude   69
Ch. 7. Initiation into Personal Discernment: The "Ignatian Day" 81
Ch. 8. The Public Life: Contemplations on Gospel Events and
        Simultaneous Deliberations about an Election   95
Ch. 9. The Third and Fourth Weeks: An Experience of Sharing in
        the Paschal Mystery   107

PART III. PROLONGATIONS OF THE EXPERIENCE OF THE EXERCISES

Ch. 10. Life in the Spirit after the Exercises Have Ended   125
Ch. 11. Prolongations of the Retreat Experience in a Personalized
         Manner   135
Ch. 12. Applying One's Personal Experience in a Communitarian Way 141

REFERENCE MATTER

Bibliography   155
Detailed Table of Contents   157

EDITOR'S FOREWORD

————————

In this book Father Gilles Cusson presents a directory for the Spiritual Exercises as made in everyday life. He discusses the structure and procedures of these "open retreats" in a way helpful to directors and retreatants.

But he also does far more. Within the framework of the open retreat he concretely applies the biblical interpretation of St. Ignatius' *Exercises* which he expounded in the 400 pages of his previous book *Biblical Theology and the Spiritual Exercises* (St. Louis: The Institute of Jesuit Sources, 1988). In many ways the present short book is a summary of the earlier long one.

When St. Ignatius' Exercises are made in everyday life, they are adjusted to the needs of one who desires spiritual progress but is not free to withdraw into the ideal circumstances, thirty days of complete solitude. Instead, he or she daily devotes an hour or so to Ignatius' nearly 150 prayerful contemplations, and thus spreads them out through something like five or six months. The ideal procedure, the "closed retreat," is described by Ignatius in the twentieth "annotation" or introductory explanation in his book (*Spiritual Exercises*, [20]). The second procedure, the "open retreat," is treated in the nineteenth annotation (ibid., [19]). Hence it is often referred to as "a nineteenth-annotation retreat."

In Part I, on the method in general, Cusson surveys the history of these open retreats in daily life. They were extensively employed by St. Ignatius and the early Jesuits but somehow dwindled away during the seventeenth century. In the past few decades, however, they have been revived and are spreading widely. Cusson next takes up techniques useful in directing or making an open retreat, such as the selection of candidates, their preparation for a profitable retreat experience, ways of giving them an overview of the road to be traveled, the difficulties, and how they may be surmounted with individuals or groups. In Part II, on the evolution of the retreatant's experience, he presents the chief exercises in the light of biblical theology. That is, the tenor of thought in the exemplifying explanations is the same as that found in the author's longer volume. In Part III he suggests means toward prolonging the retreat experience into the future.

The biblical interpretation of the *Exercises* utilized in both of these books can be summarized as follows. A retreatant who makes the Ignatian

Exercises prayerfully considers the key events in God's plan of salvation —that plan which St. Paul called "the mystery of Christ."[1] Among these meditations are God's purpose in creating human beings; then, after Adam's fall, their redemption through Christ, their growth in Christ by imitating him, and finally, their glorifying God in the beatific vision and being happy by doing it. This salvation through Christ is the central theme which runs through the whole Bible and unifies all its books. The *Exercises*, therefore, are a pedagogical method to lead people toward a personal experience of this saving God. While an exercitant is prayerfully pondering the successive steps in that salvific plan, God is simultaneously offering his graces. Hence when the exercitant cooperates with them, God is actually accomplishing his plan in the retreatant's own soul.

Cusson's treatment in the present book has grown out of his extensive experience in directing open retreats and in training directors. Before and after the appearance in 1968 of the first French edition of his commentary mentioned above, he directed numerous priests, sisters, and lay persons in both closed and open retreats. He also conducted courses, study sessions, and workshops on the *Exercises* in both Americas, Africa, Asia, and Europe. He also conducted a survey—sponsored by the Ignatian Center of Spirituality in Rome—of the nature and extent of the spreading movement of nineteenth-annotation retreats. By questionnaires he obtained information about some 315 persons in twenty-two countries who had directed or made open retreats, either privately or in groups. He published the results in another book in 1976.[2] Since then the open retreats have been spreading widely throughout the world, although statistics are not available. For example, they have been intensively promoted among the worldwide lay organization, the Christian Life Communities. And at least five of the American Jesuit provinces have encouraged their members to make them as part of province programs for renewal.

In the preceding book, *Biblical Theology and the Spiritual Exercises*, various circumstances made some adaptations of the French original to the circumstances and thought patterns of our English-speaking readers desirable.[3] The same adaptations were found advisable also in the present volume and were made with the author's kind permission. Consequently the respective roles of the two translators were somewhat different. Sister Mary Angela competently produced the basic translation and this second

---

1 E.g., in Rom. 16:25, Eph. 1:8-10 and Col. 2:2, 3. He describes this mystery enthusiastically in Eph. 3:1-21.
2 *Les Exercices dans la vie courante: Résultats d'une enquête (1966-1976)*, published by the Ignatian Center of Spirituality, Borgo S. Spirito 5, 00195 Rome, Italy.
3 See *Biblical Theology and the Spiritual Exercises*, pp. ix-x.

translator and editor made the adaptations, for which he is responsible if error has somewhere crept in. Similarly, too, the same policy as in the earlier volume has been used in the effort to avoid discriminatory language.[4]

The Institute of Jesuit Sources is happy to make this book available in English. This joy, however, is also tinged with sadness. When this book was on the point of printing, news came that the first translator, Sister Mary Angela Roduit, died on November 24, 1988, in Rome, before she could see the published result of her labor. May she from her now better life see this book, through God's providence, carry on her dedicated work on earth for many years to come.

George E. Ganss, S.J.
Director Emeritus
The Institute of Jesuit Sources
December 8, 1988

4 Ibid., pp. x and 52, fn. 22.

AUTHOR'S INTRODUCTION

The book which I am presenting here and which might easily take on the aspect of a "Directory for the Spiritual Exercises Made in Everyday Life," is not primarily intended to be an answer to a problem of technique. Its purpose, rather, is to respond to a problem that is much deeper in the life of many people today. I refer to those persons whose faith long ago had rich sources, even though they may now seem obscure. In their difficult spiritual journey, they find, their onetime fervent aspirations in life have been so often contradicted by their experiences of daily living, and they think with regret that their fervor has cooled and their motivations have become dull. It is of this journey that I wish to speak. Its demands are those of a road that cannot be left to chance. A deeply rooted renewal of fervor is what such a person desires. I would like to point out a route for this journey in the light of the experiences of our ancestors in the faith —a route which has often led to a reinvigorated spiritual life.

My own experience of accompanying others on their spiritual journey in recent years has allowed me to verify the deep yearning of modern men and women. Both the young and the not so young have a sensitivity for those interior pathways whose truth they have learned and which now challenge the truth of their own experience. This challenge is somewhat like an arduous dawn slowly rising in the human heart. The promise of approaching light wrests it from sleep and the shadows of night. It is the promise of a day when the sun will truly shine for those who are willing to open their eyes.

However, the paths laid out for a person's pilgrimage are not easy. Smooth ways would disappear as quickly as a mirage fades when one draws near to it. Beyond the apparent facility with which modern man seeks various comforts, he has the extraordinary ability to respond to this spiritual yearning which comes from the very depths of his being. He wants to be in tune with the rhythm of life, rather than to expect from structures and techniques the fancied efficiency of fruit all ready to be eaten.

That is why he or she is willing, at the age of eighteen, twenty-five, thirty, forty, or fifty, to travel once more the road called "the school of the heart." Here her or his faith can rediscover its youthful roots of former years, still moist and full of promise. Some new and necessary structures, techniques, and "laws" are then welcomed because they answer the very demands of love and of life, enabling them to flourish.

For this reason, one agrees to go back to this school where the heart and the Spirit of God meet. He or she agrees to travel the difficult and sometimes lengthy road of our hassled lives, stretching from "the law and the prophets" to the village of Emmaus, to the meal of friendship which nourishes us eternally.

The Exercises in daily life do not offer an easy way, and yet they are within the reach of anyone who wishes to learn how to lead his or her life in union with God in all that one does. They make use of the daily bread of our existence to educate our heart and our faith, to open us up to the action of the Spirit, to help us experience the friendship of the Lord. These Exercises do not ignore each person's existential situation—the burden of one's more or less integrated psychological functioning; one's social relationships with the people with whom one lives and works; and the constant need to renew one's interior covenant with a "jealous God," a "dangerous God," who loves each one to the point of folly. These Exercises are a "road to freedom" which people willingly undertake in order to become, in the silence that re-creates us, sons and daughters of the Father, brothers and sisters, and servants of Life.

> For God sent the Son into the world,
> not to condemn the world,
> but that the world might be saved
> through him (John 3:17).

Gilles Cusson

THE EXERCISES MADE IN EVERYDAY LIFE

PART I
GENERAL INFORMATION

THE TEXT OF THE NINETEENTH ANNOTATION
OF ST. IGNATIUS' *SPIRITUAL EXERCISES*

[19]. One who is educated or talented, but engaged in public affairs or necessary business, should take an hour and a half daily for the Spiritual Exercises. First, the end for which man is created should be explained to him, then for half an hour the Particular Examination of Conscience may be presented, then the General Examination of Conscience, and the method of confessing and of receiving Holy Communion. For three days, let him meditate each morning for an hour and a half on the first, second, and third sins (*Spiritual Exercises*, [45-54]). For three more days, at the same time, he should take the meditation on personal sins ([55-61]). Then for three days, at the same hour, he should meditate on the punishment due to sin ([65-71]). Along with all these meditations, he should be given the ten Additional Directions ([73-89]). In the mysteries of the life of our Lord, the same order should be observed which is explained later on in the *Exercises* themselves.

ABBREVIATIONS USED IN THE FOOTNOTES

Corso	*IV Corso Internazionale per Direttori: "Gli Esercizi ignaziani per il cristiano di oggi"* (1972)
DirSpEx	*Directoria Exercitiorum Spiritualium (1540-1599)* (1955). In MHSJ
FN	*Fontes Narrativi*, 4 volumes in MHSJ
Ledrus	*Thèmes pour les Exercices spirituels*, by Michel Ledrus
MHSJ	Monumenta Historica Societatis Iesu, the series of critically edited historical sources of the Jesuits, 129 volumes
SpEx	The *Spiritual Exercises* of St. Ignatius
*SpEx*MHSJ	Exercitia Spiritualia S. Ignatii...et Directoria (1919), in MHSJ

THE HISTORY OF "NINETEENTH–ANNOTATION RETREATS"

For those who are in any way familiar with the *Spiritual Exercises*[1] of St. Ignatius of Loyola, the text and their centuries-old practice bring to mind both the "thirty-day retreat" and the other adaptations used in the tradition of "Ignatian retreats" of six, eight, or ten days. An increasingly popular practice is bringing into prominence a lesser-known use which St. Ignatius himself made of his *Exercises* with a view to a person's spiritual training outside the ordinary retreat situation. The same Exercises are made, but their use in daily life requires an adaptation which is worthy of our careful attention.

Ignatius begins his *Spiritual Exercises* with a set of twenty paragraphs which he calls *anotaciones*. In English versions this first word of his lengthy title has often been converted into a short title for all the twenty. Most often it has been translated by "Annotations," but aptly in one version as "Introductory Observations." These paragraphs furnish preliminary information helpful to directors and retreatants alike for the good progress of the retreat. They explain what the Exercises are and various procedural aids for their success. The text of annotation 19, with which this book deals, is printed on the page facing this.

However, before undertaking an analysis of this spiritual experience inserted into the ordinary daily life of the person wishing to undergo it, I think it is appropriate to go back to the primitive traditions of the Society

---

1 [Editor's note. The term "Spiritual Exercises" gives rise to many editorial problems. Throughout this book, Spiritual Exercises (in italic type) is used when the reference is chiefly to St. Ignatius' book, and Spiritual Exercises (in roman type) when it is chiefly to the activities within a retreat. However, since his book usually envisages these activities and vice versa, there are overlappings of emphasis which often make the choice of typeface somewhat arbitrary.

To make references easier, in editions since 1928 a number in square brackets has been added to each paragraph of Ignatius' text, e.g., [21]. In references run into the text, e.g., "as is stated in *SpEx*, ([91])," the parentheses ( ) indicate that the numbers are a reference and the square brackets that the numbers themselves are an addition to the text.]

of Jesus in order to discover the origins of this fruitful practice. The reader who is not interested in the historical origins of this adaptation may, without inconvenience, skip this chapter and proceed to what follows. The ensuing chapters will describe the method proposed and give an interpretation of the Exercises adapted to the religious experience of men and women today.

Those who speak of making St. Ignatius' Spiritual Exercises "in daily life" or in "everyday life," usually make reference to "annotation 19" (*SpEx*, [19]) among his introductory explanations. There Ignatius extends the possibility of making even the full Exercises to those who cannot withdraw from everyday life for a "closed retreat" of thirty days.

With this annotation 19 in mind, I should like to begin by retracing the practice of using this manner of giving the Exercises, especially as was done in St. Ignatius' lifetime and during the first century of the Society, that is, from the years following Ignatius' conversion in 1521 down to the time of Aquaviva, whose official Directory came out in 1599. Then we shall take a brief glance at the following centuries, stopping again in our own day.[2]

A. In St. Ignatius' Own Practice (1521-1556)

At least four facts refer us to this practice of the Exercises during the life of St. Ignatius. The first is the mention in the text itself of this way of giving the Exercises. Annotations 18, 19, and 20 (*SpEx*, [18, 19, 20]), in fact, distinguish among the different categories of retreatants, and they

---

2   The documents which enable us to retrace the practice of the Exercises are the following: the Monumenta Ignatiana, the section of the Monumenta Historica Societatis Iesu which contains the volumes on St. Ignatius. Those which deal with the *Spiritual Exercises* and their various Directories are volumes 57 (1919), 76 (1955), and 100 (1969). Much material on the *Exercises* is also found in *Fontes Narrativi*, volumes I and II, in the *Memoriale* of Gonçalves da Câmara in *FN*, I, and in the French translation of the Collection "Christus" (1966); finally, in the works of the historians Pedro de Leturia, *Estudios Ignacianos* (Rome, 1957), 2 volumes, and Ignacio Iparraguirre: *Práctica de los Ejercicios de San Ignacio de Loyola en vida de su Autor (1522-1556)* (Rome, 1946), and *Historia de los Ejercicios de San Ignacio (1556-1599)*, (Rome, 1955). Along the same line is the paper of J. P. Van Schoote, read at the Congress of Loyola in August 1966 and entitled "Une formule audacieuse de grande retraite: les Exercices spirituels selon la dix-neuvième annotation" ("An Audacious Formula for the Long Retreat: The Spiritual Exercises according to the Nineteenth Annotation"). A Spanish translation of this paper, with the title "Los Ejercicios de San Ignacio según la anotación 19," appeared in *Los Ejercicios de San Ignacio a la luz del Vaticano II* (Madrid: Biblioteca de Autores Cristianos, 1968).

affirm the principle of the necessary adaptation of the Exercises.

Annotation 18 suggests some "easier" or "lighter" exercises for those who are not capable of more; in general, this refers to the exercises of the First Week. Annotation 20, on the contrary, concerns retreatants who are able to free themselves to withdraw into solitude and make the full thirty days, observing all the rules and annotations. Such retreats in solitude, of whatever duration, are ordinarily called "closed retreats." Between these two extremes is inserted the group to whom annotation 19 offers another method of making the Exercises, in part or in full. Those in this group cannot withdraw from their regular occupations; yet they desire to undergo the spiritual experience offered by the Exercises, even within the framework of their daily life. Such retreats are often called "open" retreats.

It is almost always in connection with these three annotations that the Directories of the Society's first century speak of the flexibility of the *Exercises*, of the necessity of adapting them to the retreatants, and of their suitability for being presented in ordinary life to persons who fit themselves to make them. All this is according to the intention of Ignatius.

As a second fact we have the allusion in the *Autobiography* which seems to refer rather clearly to this practice of the "open" Exercises in the life of Ignatius. In fact, the *Autobiography*[3] tells us of Ignatius' custom of going to visit his various retreatants in Rome (especially, according to Pedro de Leturia and Ignacio Iparraguirre, between the years 1538 and 1540). The reason for this is that for these particular Exercises the retreatants remained at home. They did not "retire" from their ordinary occupations. In general, it was preferable to go to visit them rather than have them come to the parlor of the community. We shall explain the reason for this later. Thus we see Ignatius going through the city, from St. Mary Major to the Ponte Sisto, on the same day, in order to visit his retreatants.[4]

A third fact, more direct and more telling in regard to St. Ignatius' practice, is recounted in the *Memoriale* of Gonçalves da Câmara. It tells of a conversation which the minister of the Roman house had with Ignatius on April 3, 1555, on the very subject of the "open Exercises." It was on this occasion that Câmara wrote:

> By the open Exercises I mean those which are given when the person making them is not in complete retreat[5] and is satisfied with taking some time for the

---

3 *Autobiography*, no. 98.
4 Ibid.
5 "Complete retreat" here means "completely withdrawn," a "closed retreat."

meditations, while at the same time going out to take care of his occupations.[6]

In the course of this conversation, Ignatius gave some precise instructions on the method of making the election during the "open Exercises." We shall return to this point later. It was also on this occasion that Ignatius showed how this practice went back very far in his own method of giving the Exercises. In this we have the fourth fact. Ignatius told Câmara how he himself had formerly given the Exercises according to this method to one of his first companions in Paris, Simão Rodrigues, who "did not leave his place of abode and who did not practice any of the austerities, in order not to interrupt his studies and because his health was not good. Father Ignatius simply gave him the meditations."[7]

To conclude this brief survey of Ignatius' practice, if we consult the historians Leturia and Iparraguirre, we shall find clear confirmation along the same lines. Leturia tells us[8] that during his most active years Ignatius showed a preference for two forms of ministry: that of the Exercises, given privately and in full, according to annotations 19 and 20, to persons specifically chosen, and that of catechesis, this time presented to much wider audiences, especially children, and following a schema along the lines of the history of salvation (the Principle and Foundation).[9]

Ignacio Iparraguirre, in his detailed study "The Practice of the Exercises during the Life of Their Author," sums up Ignatius' position as follows:

> After having given the Exercises in various ways at Manresa, Alcalá, Barcelona, Paris, and Rome, towards the end of his life he confined himself more and more to giving the complete Exercises of one month, in retirement from everyday life, with all the annotations and rules, adapting them to the condition of certain people who could not entirely leave aside their business nor withdraw to some solitary place, in conformity with the procedure suggested in annotation 19.[10]

B. In the Era of the First Generations of Jesuits (1521-1599)

First I shall deal in a general way with the attention which was given to this practice; then I shall single out the points which were developed in greater detail in some more precise commentaries in the Directories.

---

6 *Memoriale*, no. 311, in *FN*, I, 708.

7 Ibid., no. 305, in *FN*, I, 704.

8 *Estudios Ignacianos*, I, 267.

9 *Sti. Ignatii . . . Epistolae et Instructiones*, XII, 666-673.

10 *Práctica de los Ejercicios (1522-1566)*, p. 2.

1. The General Practice

In treating of the nineteenth annotation, about ten of the Directories take up again the principle of adapting the Exercises, giving this annotation a greater or lesser importance according to the case.

Jerónimo Nadal, in his Directory (no. 25), composed for the colleges in 1561, asks that care be taken to give the Exercises strictly "according to the aptitude of the persons, in conformity with what is said in annotations 18, 19, and 20 of the same Exercises."[11]

Juan de Polanco, who died in 1576, wrote a long Directory at the same time as Nadal, stating that the Exercises can be given in four ways, based on annotations 18, 19, and 20—the third way concerning people who are engaged in affairs of everyday life.[12] We shall return to this later regarding other concrete details furnished by Polanco's Directory.

Antonio Cordeses, who entered the Society in 1547, follows Polanco's division of retreatants into four categories. The fourth, compared with the other three categories mentioned explicitly in the annotations, deals with the Exercises condensed into a much shorter period of time, namely, the Exercises of eight days.[13]

Paulus Hoffaeus, a German received into the Society in Rome by St. Ignatius in 1554, wrote his Directory between the years 1575 and 1580. He, too, mentions that category of retreatants described in the nineteenth annotation.[14]

Diego Miró lived in Rome at the time of Ignatius and was always an ardent defender of his master's ideas. He left a first draft of a Directory in which he asked that the dispositions of persons be checked in order to discover those who are "apt for the Exercises according to annotations 18, 19, and 20."[15] In his complete Directory of 1582, ch. 1, no. 4, he makes the same recommendation, and refers to the same annotations.[16] Finally—we shall come back to this—he is the one who gave the Exercises in this form to Antonio Possevino, at that time secretary to the general.

González Dávila, around 1587, in his Directory (no. 54), also refers to annotations 18 and 19 to determine the way of giving the Exercises by adapting them to circumstances.[17]

J. Blondo, an Italian from Sicily, entered the Society in 1553. In his

---

11 *DirSpEx*, p. 126.
12 Ibid., p. 280.
13 Ibid., p. 535.
14 Ibid., p. 220.
15 Ibid., p. 187.
16 Ibid., p. 371.
17 Ibid., p. 497.

Directory of 1587 (no. 23), he insists very much on this adaptation to spread out the matter of the *Exercises* over a more or less prolonged period of time according to the nineteenth annotation.[18]

Fabius de Fabiis, who entered the Society in 1567, comments on the nineteenth annotation in his Directory (nos. 14 and 15), along the same lines as the preceding Directories.[19]

Finally, two anonymous Directories follow the same line of thought with regard to the nineteenth annotation. One of them, without any title or other identification, was written between 1575 and 1580;[20] the other, called the "Short Directory," was written between 1580 and 1590.[21]

2. Some Points in Detail

While they recall in a general way the principle of adaptation which is expressed in the nineteenth annotation, the preceding Directories have, in several cases, touched on points of detail which cast some light on the practice of the Exercises made in this way, that is, in the context of the daily life of the retreatant of that period.

First of all, let us recall the precise details furnished by annotation 19, in which Ignatius enumerates some criteria of selection for this category of retreatant. He speaks of the content of these Exercises, which can be that of the "complete" cycle of the experience, and of certain demands to be maintained on the level of prayer, namely, to set aside each day about an hour and a half and to try to pray always at the same time of the day.

The Directories take up these points, but they also introduce others, such as the Election, the visit to the home, and the possibility of leaving notes with the retreatant. We shall now take a look at each of these points.

a. The Selection of Truly Apt Retreatants

With regard to the selection of retreatants, the Directories follow fairly closely Ignatius' annotations which refer first of all to the natural ability of persons and to the time they have available to pursue the experience. Fabius de Fabiis, moreover, sees in this way of giving the Exercises an application of another principle which, taking into account the rhythm of the experience, allows for the lengthening or shortening of the material

---

18 Ibid., p. 471.
19 Ibid., p. 424.
20 Ibid., p. 176, no. 20.
21 Ibid., p. 455, no. 68.

suggested by the text.[22]

b. The Contents of an "Open" Retreat

Several details are given concerning the content of the Exercises made in daily life. As in the "closed" retreat, the director may give, according to the natural ability of the retreatant, either the exercises of the First Week or the complete exercises of the four Weeks. This is what Polanco, Mercurian, Hoffaeus, de Fabiis, and the Short Directory of 1580 (no. 68), state. Polanco develops at great length the division of the content of the "open" Exercises.[23] I think his insistence shows us that he was alluding to something fairly widespread at the time.

c. The Prayer

The nineteenth annotation speaks of an hour and a half. Several Directories take up this insistence of Ignatius, but it is to make clear that this hour and a half includes mental prayer and the examens. Along the same line, Hoffaeus proposes using moderation here so that the experience may not interfere with the affairs of daily life. He adds, moreover, that these open exercises may be prolonged "for as long as they [the retreatants] desire and are capable of continuing it."[24] We find the same interpretation of an hour and a half for mental prayer and the examens in Mercurian's Directory[25] and in that of de Fabiis.[26] Aquaviva's Directory of 1599 merely states that one must be as free as possible at least during the times of prayer.[27] Finally, only the anonymous Directory of 1575 states that these "open" Exercises may be given at the rate of one, two, or three hours per day.[28]

d. The Problem of an Election

The election is a problem which rightly requires special attention when the Exercises are given in daily life. It is well known how Ignatius surrounds the election with special attention in the *Exercises*: greater silence and more complete withdrawal in order that the soul may meet its Lord more intimately and let itself be moved more directly by the

---

22 *SpEx*, [162, 209], and *DirSpEx*, p. 433.
23 *DirSpEx*, pp. 282-284, in no. 15, par. 1 to 7, and nos. 16, 17, 18.
24 *DirSpEx*, p. 220.
25 Ibid., p. 250.
26 Ibid., p. 424.
27 Directory of the Spiritual Exercises (1599), ch. 2, no. 2; in *DirSpEx*, p. 583.
28 *DirSpEx*, pp. 176-177.

Holy Spirit.[29] Thus we see Ignatius telling Câmara (*Memoriale*, no. 311) that the retreatant making the "open exercises" should "withdraw" at least for the time of the election, especially if the latter bears on an "important choice like that of a state of life." Two Directories, following Ignatius, express the same reserve, those of Polanco and Hoffaeus. However, when Polanco speaks of the content of the "open" Exercises, he does not hesitate to add that this formula should be resorted to when a more efficacious way cannot be followed, that is, when the retreatant cannot withdraw into greater solitude for the election.[30] In other words, this is the ideal, and everything possible should be done to assure it; but the experience of the election should not be abandoned if the person cannot leave his ordinary way of life. We shall return to this point when we treat the practice of the Exercises proposed according to this method, in the course of our discussion of the election in the Second Week, especially in chapter 7, B and C, below.

e. Visits to the Retreatants

In Ignatius' time it was preferable for the director to visit the retreatant of the "open exercises" at home rather than to have the latter come to the community parlor. The reason for this was for greater discretion. We must place this requirement within its context, and I think that Aquaviva's Directory helps us here. We know that this Directory, which came out in 1599, brought together, as a result of a widespread inquiry throughout the Society of that time, the many concrete traditions concerning the practice of the Exercises in the first century of the Society. On this precise point of the home visit, the Directory of 1599 states that discretion was especially necessary because of the fact that in most cases the retreatants making these open exercises were persons who held rather important positions in society, "illustrious persons":[31] cardinals, ambassadors, judges, and the like. Such persons not only should not leave their occupations, but their position imposed on them a certain discretion in their actions. Regular visits on their part to "the good Fathers" would have been regarded with suspicion. On the contrary, for "the good Fathers" to go and visit them often was not at all surprising!

---

29   See the Autograph Directory, no. 6, in *SpEx*MHSJ, p. 729.
30   Polanco's Directory, no. 16, in *DirSpEx*, p. 283.
31   Directory of the Spiritual Exercises (1599), ch. 9, no. 79; in *DirSpEx*, p. 615.

f. The Giving of Notes to the Retreatant

We know from the Autograph Directory[32] that St. Ignatius required of the person who gives the Exercises that he should know well what he is going to speak about so as to be able to dispense with the text and not have to read notes to the retreatant. Ignatius felt that the entire retreat should develop along the manner of a "spiritual conversation." With regard to these Exercises which leave the retreatant to himself or herself during a longer span of time, Mercurian's Directory states that it would be good to give the retreatant in writing the main lines of what is being proposed to him so as not to burden his memory: "To give the chief points in writing is wise practice, to prevent their slipping from memory."[33]

To conclude this brief survey of the Exercises made in everyday life during the Society's first century of existence, I should like to cite some cases or concrete examples of this practice over and above that of Simão Rodrigues, who made the Exercises in this way under the direction of Ignatius himself. Iparraguirre, in the second volume of his history of the Exercises,[34] referring to Nadal, mentions the case of several Jesuits who made the Exercises in this way, probably during the course of their studies: Jean Pluges, Simon Moya, and Léonard Nosbaum, who devoted fourteen days to the First Week, and Baltasar Betancor, who spent twenty days on it.

However, the most telling example is that of Antonio Possevino. While continuing to be secretary to Mercurian, who had become general in 1573 after Laínez and Borgia, he made the Exercises in this form under the direction of Miró. His First Week lasted exactly forty days.[35] Possevino became a great apostle of the Exercises according to this method.[36] In a letter to Bartolomeo Ricci in which he speaks of his work, he declares that in acting thus he is giving the Exercises "according to the pure manner (*puro modo*) of our Father Ignatius of holy memory." Among his many retreatants in this category, the following names are known: Jean de Frimanis, patriarch-elect of Aquila, Bishop Resca, the sixth duke of Mantua, the second duke of Savoy, Count Thaddaeus of Ferrara, Monsignor Luigi Molino, bishop of Treviso. Finally, according to a likely hypothesis of Iparraguirre, Possevino gave the Exercises in this form to no less a personage than the bishop of Geneva, St. Francis de Sales.[37] This

---

32 *SpEx*MHSJ, p. 780.
33 *DirSpEx*, p. 251, no. 45.
34 *Práctica de los Ejercicios (1556-1599)*, II, p. 281, referring to *MonNad*, I and IV.
35 Ibid.
36 Ibid., pp. 43-46.
37 Ibid., p. 46.

man of God declared later that he had found in the Exercises a "holy method, familiar to the ancient Christians but since then almost completely neglected, until that great servant of God, Ignatius of Loyola, restored its usage in our forefathers' time."[38]

3. The History of These Retreats in Later Centuries

It is a fact that after the first century of Jesuit history there is hardly any mention of this method of giving the Exercises in everyday life. This is a fact which is rather difficult to explain. Another noteworthy fact which is partly connected with this, although different from it, is the popular practice which was already spreading during the generalates of Laínez and Borgia, that of adapting the material of the *Exercises* in manuals of daily meditations. However, these books limited themselves to furnishing subject matter for daily meditation which was clearly inspired by the *Exercises*, while at the same time supplying numerous citations of texts from the Bible, the writings of saints (such as Augustine, Bernard, Bonaventure, or Gregory), as well as from the Imitation of Christ.

Luis de la Palma is the one who came closest to Ignatius' thought in this manner of inspiring daily meditation. He spread the different periods of mental prayer over several days, as they were proposed by the author of the *Exercises*: meditation, repetitions, application of the senses. But in this there was no question, strictly speaking, of a guided experience of spiritual direction or discernment.

As far as I know, the only explicit mention of the Exercises made according to the nineteenth annotation during this long period comes from the Congress of Loyola in 1966, where a report was given of the case of Armand de Pontlevoy, who entered the Society after its restoration and who gave the Exercises in this way to Donoso Cortes when the latter was ambassador in Paris.[39]

In his address at the Congress of Loyola, Jean-Pierre Van Schoote speaks of this centuries-long silence which followed the first very fruitful years of the Society, and he concludes as follows:

> He [Aquaviva] lived at the end of an evolution, at the time when the practice of the Exercises according to annotation 19, which seems to have flourished in the first days of the Society, was beginning to be lost, never again to appear, as far as we know, in the history of the Society. Was the cause

---

38 See Gilles Cusson, *Biblical Theology and the Spiritual Exercises*, p. 40, fn. 121.
39 See "Los Ejercicios de San Ignacio según la anotación 19" in *Los Ejercicios de San Ignacio a la luz del Vaticano II* (Madrid: BAC, 1968), p. 654.

perhaps a certain hardening of structures within the institution?[40]

4. Renewal of the Practice in Our Times

Our present time is witnessing the rebirth of this practice, which comes to us from the earliest years of the Society. First, we must realize that this return is part of a process of research and adaptation which opens the way for numerous experiments in the giving of the Exercises. For several years in Italy, Spain, France, India, Latin America, Canada, and the United States (to mention only those places where experiments of this sort have been brought to my attention), the Exercises have been a source of inspiration for work carried on with various groups of people. They have served to clarify the journey of persons who want to progress spiritually within the framework of sodalities of our Lady, Christian Life Communities, or groups of retreatants who spread out their experience of the Exercises over definite periods of time.

But the direct practice of the Exercises made according to the nineteenth annotation is also reviving in various places, such as Belgium and Canada.

At the Congress of Loyola in August 1966, Van Schoote from Belgium gave an address on this subject based on experiences which he had initiated with some Jesuit students and young laymen at the University of Louvain. His paper was entitled: "A Bold Formula for the Long Retreat: The Spiritual Exercises According to the Nineteenth Annotation."[41]

Several years ago, in the Jesuit Province of English-speaking Canada, Father David Asselin undertook a similar work with several Jesuit theological students; however, the illness which was to lead to his premature death forced him to abandon what promised to be a most valuable activity.

For my part, I began to give the Exercises "in daily life" during the academic year of 1965-1966. Since then I have always had several persons making the Exercises in this way usually for the space of one year (in actual practice, between eight and fourteen months). Thus, during the last six years (1966-1973) I have given the Exercises to about fifty persons of rather different ages, states of life, and professions. The retreatants were

---

40   Jean-Pierre Van Schoote, S.J., of Brussels, Belgium. His address is published in the Proceedings of the Congress at Loyola, *Los Ejercicios Espirituales . . . a la luz del Vaticano II* (Madrid: Biblioteca de Autores Cristianos, 1966), pp. 639-657. This entire article is an excellent presentation, in other words, of the material in this book.

41   Ibid.

between eighteen and forty-five years of age, and of both high school and university levels. Among them were men and women religious of several communities; Jesuit tertian fathers, scholastics, and brothers; high school and university professors; professors of catechesis and psychotherapy; priests engaged in pastoral ministries; and still others. These activities led me to prepare and to give several formation sessions on "the manner of giving the Exercises in daily life" in Canada, the United States, Italy, Switzerland, and France from July 1971 to April 1973. These sessions were in fact the origin of this book.[42]

We can, therefore, say without exaggerating that the movement of the Exercises given and made according to the nineteenth annotation is having a certain vigorous rebirth, which is linked with a distant tradition and is already finding convinced participants in several countries. We can hope for a fruitful future for this development if it is carried on seriously.

In 1966 at the Congress of Loyola, Van Schoote had said:

> The method of the nineteenth annotation gives an unsuspected breadth to the grace of the Exercises. By force of circumstances the closed retreat of thirty days remains more or less exceptional. How many people in our day can allow themselves, without too much inconvenience, the great luxury of a whole month of solitude? . . . But people are hardly aware, except in theory, . . . that Ignatius had no intention of reserving the Exercises in their entirety for those persons who enjoy extraordinary leisure. With daring and originality he earnestly wanted the busiest persons of this time, both priests and lay people, to be able to share in the specific grace of the full Exercises. It was for their benefit, as well as for ours, that he provided the nineteenth annotation, for there is certainly no shortage of very busy people today.
>
> It seems to me that the formula of the long retreat according to the nineteenth annotation, so easy from some points of view, is like the gentle breeze which hides the presence of the living God before whom the prophet hid his face. I may be wrong, but I am inclined to see it as a providential means that is well suited to the real needs of our time.

I am dedicating this work to all those who are interested in this method of "spiritual accompaniment" directly inspired by the *Exercises* and who are willing to devote a certain regular time for "the good of souls," as St. Ignatius loved to repeat. It is an attempt to harvest the fruit of actual experiences and to place them at the disposition of all those who give the

---

42 A statistical survey, later and still more abundant, on the present growth of the "Exercises in Everyday Life" is in Gilles Cusson, *Les Exercices dans la vie courante: Résultats d'une enquête (1966-1976)*, (Rome: Ignatian Center of Spirituality, 1976).

Exercises, so as to help them discover and use this way of interior conversion to the following of the one Master, Jesus.

———————

Chapter 2

THE METHOD IN GENERAL

In the whole of the work which follows I intend to propose, and not to impose. Nothing should be taken as an absolute norm, even if statements are sometimes made with a certain insistence. On the other hand, whatever I shall say, I have drawn from my own experience, during which the "rules of the game" have been progressively imposed on me. I am convinced that others might experience and describe the same procedure with substantially different nuances. Hence, what I say on the subject has value only within my own experience of "accompaniment."

A. Some Practical Details

First, I should like to answer certain questions which arise spontaneously when we speak of the Exercises "made in daily life," that is, the length of time given to the experience for each person and the frequency of the interviews necessary for its realization.

I have almost always given the full Exercises privately, that is, to each person individually. These experiences have lasted for the space of a year —an academic year for some (eight or nine months), and a full year for others (between ten and fourteen months). During this time the person made the Exercises, usually meeting the director once a week.

The weekly meeting was considered necessary in most cases. These interviews assure a genuine continuity in the person's spiritual journey, and are especially necessary at the beginning as a help to commitment since there are no other special conditions to sustain it. There were a few exceptions to holding the meetings weekly, and I can say that in these cases a difference was clearly perceptible.[1]

---

1   Here I am not speaking about the case of the Jesuits. During their tertianship they must devote an especially intensive month to this experience of the Exercises. In this context the making of the Exercises in daily life does not require the same limiting conditions of solitude as those required for the Jesuits. But there is just as much profit in submitting to the regular control of the director.

Later in this chapter I shall come back to the content of the weekly interview. This will give the opportunity more clearly to discern its role and to evaluate better the progress the retreatant is making.

B. The Candidates for the Exercises Made in Everyday Life

1. Their Selection

For this form of the Exercises it is sufficient to use the same criteria that St. Ignatius proposes for the choice of retreatants capable of making the long retreat. Briefly, it is a question of persons who have a certain capacity for spiritual awareness, who, within the limits of their spiritual interest and their correspondence with grace, are capable of committing themselves progressively to cooperating with God in accomplishing his plan of creation, redemption, and glorification, a plan called by St. Paul the "mystery of Christ." This is the spirit of "the more" or "the greater" (*magis*) translated into the language of today. It presupposes serious motivation, expressed by a mature spiritual desire, as well as by a human balance which leaves sufficient freedom for a commitment to a demanding spiritual journey. We shall come back to these questions when we speak of a "preparatory stage" for the Exercises made in daily life.

Therefore, it is very important for the director to know the person who wishes to begin these Exercises, his or her motivations and capacities, in order to foresee in some way the likelihood of his or her seriously embarking on an undertaking which will gradually be marked by the very radicality of the Gospel. From what was said in the preceding chapter, it is apparent that today on all levels of Christian life there are persons desirous and capable of living to the full their Christian commitment by means of a greater enlightenment in faith and of a more complete integration on all levels of existence—students of both sexes, laypersons, religious, and priests.

2. The Requirements

With regard to this manner of giving the Exercises, we might say that the criteria of choice can be reduced to a few basic requirements which should be stated at the beginning of the experience. In practice, there are three requirements, and I present them to the person who is about to make the Exercises, while trying to discover if they already exist in his or her life.

In order to carry out this experience concretely, I must first of all know that the exercitant is a person who is capable of sustained reflection, of a sort of interior preoccupation, even in the midst of his or her ordinary life. For here there is question of making the Exercises within the framework of that everyday life. This obviously requires a minimum capacity of rather spontaneous concentration on some matter for serious reflection. I express this activity in more concrete terms by asking the person if he or she feels capable of living with an interior preoccupation, of keeping it rather frequently in mind, of coming back to it occasionally in all sorts of circumstances. It is then possible to see if this person has discovered or is likely to discover this aptitude of sustaining within himself or herself, over not-yet-determined periods of time, one or more considerations—independently, here, of their more or less spiritual content. Here we must discern the person's capacity for the type of activity which the experience undertaken requires. In other words, it is essential that he or she be capable of being engrossed in a problem, of letting the mind dwell on it, so that one learns to live with it, to become familiar with it. This is probably the most important natural aptitude for the Exercises made in daily life.

Secondly, I ask the person about the possibility of finding some minutes at least once each day in order to pause and to reflect directly on the subject matter of the exercise in question. This pause can be called meditation, but I prefer to make a distinction between it and the period (perhaps an hour or so) of prayer properly so called, to which it can be linked with profit.

That is why I require that, in the third place, the pause for reflection always end with a certain time of prayer so that the activity of this "open" retreat may not remain merely on an intellectual level, but rather that it may become the occasion of a genuine meeting and conversation with God. Such activity is altogether necessary for the aim, a vivid spiritual experience.

These are the three requirements which I make of the person who wishes to follow the Exercises with me.

To sum up, I should say that these basic aptitudes are needed: (1) a spiritual intelligence suitable for opening oneself to the light of faith and (2) a spiritual desire which is serious and engrossing. In addition, I look for the intention and will to nourish daily the preoccupation with the faith experience, by means of a few minutes or pauses given to reflection and prayer. However, I must say that I have never taken it upon myself to impose fixed boundaries for these periods of meditation, prayer, and reflection, demanding, for example, such and such a minimum. I think, too, that my experience up to now has proven that I am right. It is for the persons concerned progressively and concretely to learn from their own experience, to discover for themselves their pace of prayer, their manner of reflecting, and the like. I have noticed that they always began by giving far less time than that prescribed in the directories, but that gradually and of themselves they approached the norm and often went beyond it. Today it is absolutely necessary to have a fundamental respect for this rhythm of time and for the maturity of the person. Retreatants should be encouraged to discover through an interior movement the concretization of the essentials of growth in faith, demands which I recall in general terms and which I propose as indispensable conditions. I do this by means of the few requirements which I lay down at the outset. Today precise "calculations" imposed from without not only hamper the spirit, but can also harm the true élan of personalized spiritual experience.

3. The Remote Preparation of the Candidates

Here we must speak of two periods of preparation for the Exercises, the remote and the proximate. These two periods are extremely important for all the rest of the experience.

To the remote preparation I devote a variable period of time as needed for each case. The needs are of two orders. They concern, on the one hand, the knowledge which the director must acquire of the retreatant and, on the other, the maturity of the retreatant with regard to the aptitudes already mentioned—sufficient balance, an open spiritual intelligence, maturity of desire and of his or her underlying motivations.

In fact, a director should take the time required to know as well as possible the person who is committing himself or herself to an experience of this kind. Who is he? Who is she? What is he? What is she? Where does he or she come from? How has he or she become this particular person? How does he or she live? What inspires or impedes him or her? This is necessary in order to insure the quality of the experience which will follow and which should be a true continuation of the spiritual life history of this person and of his or her evolution in the Spirit. With this in mind, the "accompaniment" which the director proposes should be adapted to the laws of this particular life story, of which he or she must, as it were, take possession along with the retreatant.

This period of "getting acquainted" helps to understand the second stage, namely, to progress towards that maturity which is necessary on the various levels already mentioned: that of balance which leaves room for sufficient freedom, that of spiritual openness expressed in the capacity for wholehearted acceptance in faith, and that of a consistent and committed interior desire.

To the degree that the persons presenting themselves are more or less free, mature, or ready for these different levels of demands that are being made, this stage of remote preparation takes a longer or shorter time to achieve its aim. In practice, for me this has varied from a few weeks, that is, several interviews, to a whole year of general spiritual direction, intended to help the person acquire the right dispositions for the experience.

4. The Proximate Preparation

a. Its Sequence

The immediate preparation takes place just before the beginning of the Exercises. This introduction, which can be made in one or two interviews, is a direct initiation into the experience we are undertaking. It embraces the progressive unfolding of thought proposed by the book of *Exercises*, the interactions of factors in Christian living, the basic dispositions which follow from these for beginning the Exercises, and the overall vision of the spiritual journey to be made. After this, the concrete requirements are gone over—a reflective consciousness and a time for quiet—in an attempt to see their importance in the conduct of the experience we are undertaking. Finally, we decide how frequent the interviews should be and how they are to be conducted, two factors which must always be adapted to persons and circumstances.

b. Its Content

For what concerns the content of this immediate preparation, its general line of thought, procedure, dispositions, comprehensive view of the whole, and dialectical interactions, I refer the reader to my earlier book, *Biblical Theology and the Spiritual Exercises: A Method toward a Personal Experience of God as Accomplishing within Us His Plan of Salvation*.[2] The most important considerations relevant here are those on the dialectical interactions between the universal or general and the particular. These considerations will govern all the coming activity of director and retreatant, that on the objective level of the thought content communicated and, on the subjective level, of the exercitant's reactions to it.[3] Also important for the relation of the universal and the particular in Ignatius' own life are the sections in chapter 2, on his worldview and on his conceptions of God, the universe, and the human person with his or her particular vocation.[4]

To this abundant material of initiation, of which only the elements are

2 *Biblical Theology and the Spiritual Exercises*, pp. 80-117.
3 Ibid., pp. 94-98.
4 Ibid., pp. 52-67.

enumerated immediately above, I should like to add two points which I feel are also important and on which my own experience has led me to place special emphasis during this stage of immediate preparation: (1) an accurate understanding of the experience sought and its relation to the previous experience of the retreatant and (2) an overall view of what is to come.

c. An Understanding of the Experience

First I wish to insist that the spiritual experience we are embarking upon should be understood in a relative sense so as to keep it within its true limits. This will avoid pretentiousness without in any way diminishing the absolute character of its demands.

We are dealing here, not with a spiritual experience of initiation, but rather with one of deepening. This means that we are not starting from zero; instead, we are taking previous experiences into consideration and incorporating them into the present. Hence, it is in the continuity of a concrete spiritual history—"my history of salvation," "the history of my faith," "the history of God in my life" (of which the person will take possession little by little)—that this new in-depth experience will take place. All the bases of the spiritual experience are there, already contained in the person and in his or her history, which is already one element of God's plan of salvation and spiritual development for him. What must be done is to learn how to graft on to those past experiences a process of deepening which aims at going much further, right up to the limit of one's possibilities of response to God, in light and in generosity.

d. An Overall View of the Coming Retreat

Secondly, I do not begin this deepening process without giving a general idea of the road which we shall follow. In this matter it is important to take Ignatius' remark seriously, that while we are making one stage of the Exercises we should not encroach on the stages still to come. This does not mean that there is something to hide and that we should pretend suddenly to discover new elements in God's revealed plan of salvation, some elements unsuspected before any given topic for meditation or contemplation was suggested. Rather, it means that during the time of living out the experience, one should concentrate on one stage at a time, in order to live out that stage as fully as possible in the present moment. In order to be moved in an intelligent way toward these complementary stages, it is important to undertake the journey in the light which the procedure as a whole throws on the details of the individual stages, one by one as they come. We must be able to accept this light of faith so as to desire to live by it in a more interior, more intense way. We are not called upon to walk blindly in the following of Christ. It seems to me that the overall view of the road to be followed, proposed in this way, will always be active. It carries within it a motivating power which is often decisive.

i. With Emphasis on the Objective Level

Various ways of giving the overall preview of the coming procedure are possible. Often, for example, a director simply takes Ignatius' own divisions and headings in the book of the *Exercises* and by means of them explains the sequence of thought in the chief topics of the four Weeks. This is done first on the objective level of the thought to be communicated. Then the director moves to the subjective level of the exercitant's experience and explains what reactions each Week and its chief topics ordinarily stimulate. This manner of presentation is indicated schematically in Figure 1, on the next page.

ii. With Emphasis on the Subjective Level

However, it is possible to analyze and divide the *Exercises* in another way and in different terms, in order to put more emphasis on the interior experience of the exercitant and its progressive development. In my practice I have grown more and more inclined to do this. To Ignatius' divisions (which remain accurate and clarifying) I add an analysis of the expected experience, presented as a journey on a road to be traveled in stages. In this way I treat the experience more concretely and more from the viewpoint of the retreatants.

Thus they see that their expected spiritual experience will come in successive stages which advance from what is universal or general to what is more particular. That is, the sequence begins with God's plan of creation, redemption, and glorification in general, and then moves into the particular, namely, into the events in the life of Christ and the lessons which can be learned from them. Thus, as the exercitants continue their journey stage by stage, their attention is continually brought back to that global plan, and they see each event in the light of it. The very journey stimulates them to insert themselves cooperatively into that divine plan for spiritual growth as it is unfolding in history. Further still, they are encouraged to live there with realism, the realism which pays attention to details. Let me explain.

Ignatius' *Exercises* can be divided into two main sections, through each of which the retreatant's journey is made in three stages. Those in section I consist of (1) the Principle and Foundation, which gives the overall perspective arising from God's plan of salvation and spiritual growth; (2)

Figure 1: St. Ignatius' Divisions of the *Exercises*

OBJECTIVE LEVEL of the thought proposed		SUBJECTIVE LEVEL of our reactions to it
The unifying outlook of Christian faith	THE FOUNDATION	Fundamental attitude of seeing all things from this viewpoint
Sin: in general my personal sins God's saving love	FIRST WEEK	Awareness of our spiritual poverty Experience of Christian hope
Christ and his mission Christian's participation	SECOND WEEK THE KINGDOM	The King and His Kingdom Offering of oneself
Infancy and hidden life: Christ the Savior	HIDDEN LIFE	To contemplate, learn Desire to grow in him
The Two Standards The Three Classes The Three Degrees	THE IGNATIAN DAY	Initiation to personal discernment: our openness, and matter for an election
From the Baptism to Palm Sunday Proclamation of the word, accompanied by the Holy Spirit	THE PUBLIC LIFE	Contemplation-election Hearing and accepting the word preached Accepting the Spirit's action Devising my response
From the Last Supper to the establishment of the Church Christ's salvific action: personal, universal, continuing	THIRD AND FOURTH WEEKS THE PASCHAL MYSTERY	Uniting oneself with this action: to consent fully, by the the election, to death and resurrection in union with Him A Yes to be continually renewed
Ignatius' help toward cultivating the fruit of the Exercises	CONTEMPLATION TO ATTAIN LOVE FOR GOD	Faith's intuition, focused on love, to increase our love

First Week, what evil has done and still does to that plan; and (3) the Kingdom, a bird's-eye view of Christ's mission and a transition to the next section. The stages in section II present Christ as Savior. They are (4) the exercises connected with the hidden life in the context of Christ's mission; (5) his public life, with contemplations on its events and with parallel meditations preparatory for a possible election; and (6) our association with him in his paschal mystery.

In section I, stages 1, 2, and 3 advance in the realm of the universal. They offer to the exercitant the outlook of Christian faith. This worldview becomes increasingly inspiring and captivating in the Foundation, and then in the First Week it reveals the heinousness of sin and evil, the attempts to thwart the divine plan. In section II, by contrast, stages 4 and 5 (in the Second Week) and 6 (in the Third and Fourth Weeks) are very different in the rhythm of their development, which goes into minute details. These three stages are devoted to our assimilation of God's salvific plan—this "mystery of Christ"[5] as it unfolds before our eyes at its high point in the history of salvation, that is, during the lifetime of Christ. That salvific plan is prayerfully studied in detail, with precision and even exegetical exactitude. Meanwhile the exercitant is inserting herself or himself into God's plan by accepting his role in it amid the concrete realities of daily life. These two sections—the first, exposition along with growing awareness, and the second, assimilation with self-integration—are mutually complementary. Both are needed to ensure the genuine and realistic Christian spiritual experience.

Now let us see how these two sections with their six stages enable us to regroup the content of the *Exercises*, both on the objective level of doctrine and method, and on the subjective level of the retreatant's experience.

Section I of the experience will include the Foundation, the First Week, and the contemplation on the Kingdom. In stage 1, the Foundation imparts (on the objective level of the message communicated) the global

---

5 [Editor's note. For a brief global view of God's plan of creation, redemption, spiritual growth, and salvation in the beatific vision, see the bird's-eye view presented by means of a sequence of Scripture texts in *Biblical Theology and the Spiritual Exercises*, pp. 342-344. On "the mystery of Christ," the term used by St. Paul to describe it (e.g., in Rom. 16:25-27; Ephes. 1:9-12; 3:4; Col. 2:2), see ibid., pp. 335-344. Throughout chapter 3 of Ephesians, St. Paul writes enthusiastically of this mystery of Christ and its inspiring ramifications. The mystery of Christ is the theme which runs through all the books of the Bible and links them into a unity. It is also the theme which unifies all the parts in many a Christian classic, such as St. John's Gospel and First Epistle, St. Augustine's *City of God*, St. Thomas Aquinas' *Summa of Theology*, or St. Ignatius' *Spiritual Exercises*.]

outlook arising from Christian faith. It is the fundamental principle in whose light all the subsequent topics are to be viewed. In stage 2, this outlook of faith is more clearly and realistically understood when the exercitant views what sin has done and still does to God's plan in its gradual evolution on earth, and further views the problem of evil with that divine plan as the background. In stage 3, a transition to the next section, the retreatant, still drawing on that global outlook, focuses directly on Christ. By taking his part, in cooperation with his Father, in the divine plan, he made supernatural salvation available again to humankind; and he invites each exercitant—including myself—by free cooperation to share in his mission, even generously, no matter what the cost.

Section II of our journey is, typically, that of a spiritual experience "according to the way of Jesus." It is based on a privileged portion of God's revelation, the gospel message brought by Christ. This inspires me, as exercitant, to insert its multiple facets into my own life and thereby place myself into the moving, dynamic "mystery of Christ" (Eph. 3:1-21) which brings humankind and all the created universe to fulfillment (1 Cor. 15:21-24). In this section too there are three stages of assimilation, to which we shall return later in the book. They are wholly dominated by the very purpose of God's revelation, which exists so that humankind may have life and have it more abundantly. God's revealed plan of salvation, too, will be prominent in these three stages of assimilation: in stage 4, during the Second Week, the infancy narratives (chapters 1 and 2 in Matthew and Luke); in stage 5, the proclamation of the Word Incarnate according to the four Gospels, from the baptism in the Jordan to Christ's entrance into Jerusalem; and in stage 6, during the Third and Fourth Weeks, the paschal mystery, which begins with the Last Supper and, in the Acts of the Apostles, includes the beginning of the Church and some of its early history.

In regard to the subjective level, for both sections I and II as well as for each of the six stages into which we have analyzed the experience, the fruit is identical to what is stated within the framework of the *Exercises*, with its Foundation and its four Weeks. (The Second Week is split up, for the purposes of the subjective experience, into the divisions shown in the preceding table.) However, the plan we have drawn up has the advantage, on the subjective level, of helping the person insert himself or herself much more precisely within God's revealed plan of salvation unfolding in history. In this way one can better conform oneself to the dynamic thrust of the experience, in which God's universal plan is continually drawn upon so that the exercitant can view each particular situation in the clarifying light of the universal. The universal nourishes with its breadth of vision what is particular and limited, and personalizes it by drawing it within its limitless horizons. It sees things from God's point of view.

Once this line of development has been pointed out and proposed for the spiritual experience of the retreatant, it becomes for him or her sound theological doctrine which is rich and inspiring. In the measure in which faith becomes clarified in all its richness and splendor—this faith which is at one and the same time universal and personalized in Christ—hope takes on a new meaning. It entices the exercitant to a commitment of love which is a gift of God, to participation in a divine mission, and to service of him and one's fellow human beings. This same dynamic of a spiritual experience (now biblically and theologically understood) will be vividly present in the whole journey through the Exercises. It will also be a basis for the Contemplation to Attain Love, Ignatius' concluding suggestion for directly cultivating the fruit acquired in all the exercises of the retreat.

5. A Road to Be Traveled in Six Stages

These practical stages of the experience which is about to come in daily life follow the basic directions of the *Exercises*. Through them we shall always try to keep in touch with the guiding and directing line of the faith experience which culminates in the commitment of love. Taking account of the regrouping proposed above, and in order to emphasize the dynamic movement of the spiritual journey, I divide the subject matter of the *Exercises* into definite sections, with which the following chapters will deal one after the other. This regrouping and distribution give us the itinerary for the road which we shall travel, as presented schematically in Figure 2 on the following page.

Figure 2. Our Journey and Its Six Stages

SECTION I: EXPOSITION and DEEPENING (This gives us the outlook or worldview of Christian faith, so that we can see all things in the light of God's plan of creation and salvation.)

1st stage: The unifying vision of Christian faith, which is presented in the Principle and Foundation

2nd stage: Viewing the problem of evil against the background of God's plan of creation and salvation, in the First Week

3rd stage: Deepening of *my* Christian life, by concentrating on the "mystery of Christ," God's plan for *my* salvation, spiritual growth, and glorification, in the Kingdom (a transitional bird's-eye view of section II)

SECTION II: ASSIMILATION of and SELF-INSERTION into God's plan, by contemplating the events in the life of Christ, the Way, the Truth, and the Life, and by the election

4th stage: Christ and his saving mission
Contemplations on the Incarnation and Infancy: a prelude

5th stage: a. Initiation into personal spiritual discernment; also, introduction to the parallel contemplations on Christ and the guidelines to a sound election
The guidelines are in the Two Standards, Three Classes, and Three Modes of Humility.
b. The parallel contemplations on the public life of Christ

6th stage: Association with Christ in the paschal mystery, in the Third and Fourth Weeks
The Contemplation to Attain Love for God, by seeing him, with gratitude, in all his gifts

---

In our present study, the Contemplation to Attain Love will be dealt with in chapter 12, the last in this book. It will treat the extension of the Exercises, or rather, the spiritual experience of the Exercises, into daily living after the making of the Exercises has ended.

PART II

THE EXPERIENCE OF THE RETREATANTS
AND ITS EVOLUTION

Chapter 3

THE VIEWPOINT OF FAITH
WHICH PUTS ALL THINGS INTO A UNIFIED ORDER:
THE PRINCIPLE AND FOUNDATION

The first section of our in-depth experience consists of exercises to enable us to view all of reality—God and all his creatures—with the outlook of our Christian faith. For this to be effective it is necessary to bring into operation, on the objective level, a worldview which springs from that faith, in such a way that this vision is broad, unifying, dynamic, and personalized. Then on the subjective level that ensemble of truths will awaken and sustain an overall attitude by which we consciously view all things in the light of that faith. In this way we foster a desire to adjust ourselves realistically to the universe as it is, which we now perceive and interpret in this light of faith. We begin to insert ourselves into God's salvific plan in order to take a cooperative part in it as it unfolds in history.

Let us now look at the subject matter of this first program of training in personal spiritual experience.

A. The Objective in This First Stage

Our purpose in this first stage of section I of our journey is to cultivate an overall and fundamental attitude and faith vision which will bring about an equally basic attitude of sensitivity to this viewpoint, and of presence to all creation as viewed in this light.

When the text of the *Exercises* is taken as our guide and inspiration, we should not limit this perception of reality to the few very concise elements given in the Principle and Foundation—God, man, and all the things on the face of the earth. We should go back to the original worldview of this compelling experience in the life of Ignatius himself—the vision on the banks of the Cardoner, where the penitent of Manresa saw the whole of creation coming forth from God as from a great white light and unfolding in a development which took in all history, Christ, the Church, and Ignatius himself, called to live within the context of this light.[1] Nothing existing is outside this dynamic vision of a universe in process of being built up in God. That is why the attitude flowing from it is one of respectful attention and of committed participation, cost what it may.

Here we recognize the two parts of the text of the Principle and Foundation which sets a twofold activity into motion. It would be a mistake to reduce it to a few speculative considerations on the subject which soon fade away. The first two sentences propose a contemplative activity viewing all of creation in its immensity, clarified by light from God himself. Hence, this calls for exercises of "presence" to this reality perceived in faith. The second part, the remainder of the Foundation, brings out the line of the viewer's subjective experience. He or she will graft onto it the "petition for the grace" (the search for the fruit, "that which I desire," *id quod volo*) —the grace to grow in an interior desire for cooperative fidelity to this vision. This created universe offers him the opportunity of playing a personal role in it, as unconditionally as possible (through indifference). He can share in God's plan of creation as it is gradually unfolding to its fulfillment in the Church and in the world.

The mature awareness of this twofold reality—the expanse of the divine plan with its attractive goal in which we are involved, and God's invitation to us to take our own part in it—will generate desire and a strong interior experience, which in turn often results in energetic practice. Blessed are you who hunger. You will be satisfied.

B. Guiding the Retreatant's Experience

On the objective level of the message to be communicated, a director's task is to propose the unifying vision which arises from the content of our Christian faith. That is, the director desires either to impart this unifying vision or to refresh it with its inspiring goal so that it truly guides the exercitant's activity—somewhat as Ignatius' vision beside the Cardoner dominated all his activity for the rest of his life.

On the subjective level of the retreatant's experience, her or his task is fidelity to the activities from which this vision ordinarily arises. A director's work is to accompany the retreatant and conversationally help him or her to evaluate it.

---

1 See *Biblical Theology and the Spiritual Exercises*, pp. 1-19; 23-39.

1. On the Objective Level of the Message Communicated

  a. Presenting the Worldview Which Arises from Our Christian Faith

In a certain sense we are concerned with making our own what faith tells us about the reality which surrounds us—God and all his creatures throughout the universe, things visible and invisible; the past, the present, and the future; material creation; human beings, the living and the dead; good and evil. For the vision of faith takes in everything, with nothing excluded. Everything has its place in this light which comes to us from God's revelation. That is why we can say that in the light of faith the reality of which we speak is immense, universal; that it is one, insofar as it constitutes (except for God) one single totality in the process of becoming; and that it is fully personalized in Him who sets it in motion, animates it, and brings it to fulfillment.

How can retreatants, each one for himself or herself, formulate and nourish this faith vision of all reality, the topic of this first basic activity of contemplation? There are several approaches which are useful, not only to adapt it to the mentality of the persons whom we are directing, but also to keep the inspiration alive during an experience which could last for several months when the Exercises are made in daily life.

First, we may, if we wish, use Ignatius' own language within the context of the *Exercises*. In my previous study on this subject I tried to reconstitute Ignatius' own comprehensive worldview of God, Father, Son, and Holy Spirit, of the whole of creation, the vocation of human beings, the significance of the created universe, the place of evil in it, and the necessity of ordering one's life in this light of faith.[2]

A director, to deepen his or her knowledge of all this (or a first-time retreatant, if time is available, especially after the Exercises have ended) can find still more abundant material by referring directly to the Bible. He or she can well start with the Hebrews' experience of faith. It led them step by step to an enlightened sense of created existence. The history of Israel and biblical anthropology enable us to follow that experience, which extends from Abraham to Jesus Christ, and meanwhile the content of this faith in the living God becomes progressively clearer. In the midst of a cultural context of beliefs in "gods of death," in which the myths of the "drama of creation" and of the "tragic" condition of man predominate, the Jews progressively affirmed their faith in genuine life through their experience of the God of life. The concrete experience of their living relationship to this God was the Covenant which, in essence, furnished

2 Ibid., pp. 94-99.

their confidence and hope for life for human beings and for the universe. The books recording the Covenant and its history generated their Messianic hope. Christ realizes in himself this hope of fulfillment, through his Being, his Life, and his resurrection. He is the New Adam placed at the head of the new creation who receives the nations as his inheritance, and who has the power to transmit this life to the Mystical Body which takes shape after him, recapitulating the whole universe and growing towards the plenitude of being—with the tireless patience of time.

In order to nourish this biblical vision of faith which reveals existence tending towards fullness of life as yet incomplete, we may refer to the whole of the Bible, especially Genesis, the Prophets, Job, Wisdom, and the Psalms in the Old Testament; and in the New Testament certain passages of the Gospels—John and the parables of the Kingdom in the Synoptics —and particularly the Epistles of Paul and the Apocalypse.

This is how I arrange the proposed texts in view of the dynamic theme of revelation for an experience of faith:

Experience of the Living God (in the Old Testament):

1. Wisdom 11:22-12:2, a text which summarizes the content of the Hebrew experience of the God of life. See also Wisdom 1:13-14; 2:21-24; 3:1ff; 9:1ff; 13:1ff.
2. Other texts which take up again the dynamic theme of this experience beyond the patriarchs (on the individual and the national dimension, see, e.g., Sirach 44-50). Consider especially the universalizing experience of the prophets in Isaiah 9:1-6; 11:1-9; 25:6-12; 32:14-19; 33:17-24; 35; 41:8-20; 42:1-18; 43:1-7; 44:1-8; 45:7-13,18,19; 44:1-3; 61; 66:18ff; Ezekiel 36 and 38.
3. For the period of the universalization properly so-called of the message, see Genesis 1 and 2; Job 38ff.
4. To pray this vision in the spirit of its revelation, see
    a. Psalms 8, 36, 104, 113, 145.
    b. Psalms 95, 121, 124, 126, 139.

Experience of Christ the Life (in the New Testament):

1. Acts 17:22-31; Romans 8:18ff; 1 Corinthians 3:9-17; Galatians 4:4ff; Ephesians 1:3ff; 3:8ff; Colossians 1:15ff; Hebrews 1:2; Revelation 4; 21:1ff.
2. This theme is fully developed in St. John, chapters 4, 5, 6, 15, and passim.
3. The parables of the Kingdom.

Many biblical commentaries may be used as a help to understanding the texts referred to. However, we should keep in mind that what interests us is *praying*, with these texts as a basis.[3]

Another approach which may sometimes be used, especially in order to renew one's inspiration as the experience progresses during this first stage, is the vision proposed by Teilhard de Chardin in the book describing his faith.[4] This viewpoint is another expression of the same cosmic, personalized, and evolving reality—but in a different language which often suits people of today in an existential and very positive sense. Other writings of Teilhard may be used for the same purpose.[5]

Obviously, several other authors might be consulted if necessary and according to the inspiration of the retreatant. I do not intend to be exhaustive in this matter, but rather to suggest helps which I have found valuable in my own experience. With this in mind I shall add two well-known names, von Balthasar and Evdokimov. Throughout this experience I often propose Hans Urs von Balthasar's splendid book *Heart of the World*.[6] The first chapter entitled "The Kingdom" affords, after one has spent some time in the exercise, a reprise of the foundational vision in an engaging movement of interiorization. Finally, for the Principle and Foundation we can find abundant and very contemplative subject matter in the first six chapters of Part One of *L'Art de l'icône, Théologie de la beauté* by Paul Evdokimov, which gives a biblical vision of Beauty, a theology of Beauty from the Fathers and others.[7]

After drawing on these different sources—biblical, Ignatian, Teilhardian, and others—there is more to do. In order to further deepen the faith vision that can inspire one to understand and accept *present reality*, one must take careful account of *present actuality* inasmuch as it is material

3 Among other books which I recommend within this context of interpretation, there are the following: Edmond Jacob, *Le Dieu Vivant*, Foi Vivante, no. 137 (Paris: Seuil, 1971); D. Stanley, *A Modern Scriptural Approach to the Spiritual Exercises*, chs. 1-5, for his commentaries on Isa. 43:1-7; Pss. 95; 121; 114; 8:2-10; 126. A Foundation is worked out from several of the texts referred to above, from Gen., Pss., Rom., Eph., and John, in Laplace, *The Plan of God and the Response of Man*, pp. 35-46. Also useful are John McKenzie, *Dictionary of the Bible* (Milwaukee, 1973), s.v. "mystery," pp. 597-598, and X. Léon-Dufour, *Dictionary of Biblical Theology* (New York, 1973), s.v. "Plan of God," pp. 432-435.
4 Pierre Teilhard de Chardin, *How I Believe* (New York, 1969).
5 Pierre Teilhard de Chardin, *Mon Univers* (Paris: Seuil, 1965); *Réflexions et prières dans L'espace-temps* (Paris: Seuil, 1972); *The Divine Milieu* (New York: Harper and Row, 1960). See also his prayer of the vision of the universe, accepted in faith, as he so well expresses it in his *Hymn of the Universe* (New York, 1965).
6 H. U. v. Balthasar, *Heart of the World* (San Francisco: Ignatius Press, 1979).
7 Paul Evdokimov, *L'art de l'icône: Théologie de la Beauté* (Paris, 1970).

altogether appropriate to this Principle and Foundation exercise. The retreatant should not be content merely to draw from present realities some inspiration for prayer. She or he should also carefully examine them in the light of faith, which envisions incarnation of this sort. In other words, the retreatant must be helped to find in revelation the habitual attitude and outlook which will inspire his daily life in his own concrete reality: in his own self, in the persons he meets, in the events of his life, in the dispositions he experiences, and the like. This interpretation of existence which is accepted in prayerful faith is to be applied to the life of every day during and after the retreat. This is the primary objective of the Foundation and of the retreat itself—a sort of spiritual apprenticeship.

2. On the Subjective Level of the Retreatant's Experience

a. Explaining the Procedure to Be Used

Once this subject matter of the Foundation has been proposed, we come to the stage of the practical application which we may call the stage of apprenticeship, training, or learning. This exercise consists in making an effort, by means of reflection in daily life, by reflection during moments of pause or quiet, and by a period devoted explicitly to prayer, in order to live in the present and to be aware of this dimension which concerns every reality that I meet, touch, know, experience, or undergo. Making use of the grace God offers for this, I must make an effort to live habitually on the level of this interpretation of reality by means of faith. I must not only have recourse to it occasionally, for example, in times of difficulty or trial, while the rest of the time being influenced by temporal considerations and superficial judgments. I must learn to take my stand on this level of existence and from this standpoint meet every reality, by seeing, loving, and judging in this light which reveals to me the true meaning of reality. In this way I must develop a second reflex which is just as spontaneous as a natural reflex but which makes me react constantly within the vision of faith.

Hence, the exercise has a definite purpose—to learn to live out one's faith vision—first in a global way, as a basic attitude of presence to life as perceived from this viewpoint of faith, in all the circumstances of my existence.

b. Evaluating the Experience

The weekly interview gives us the opportunity to verify whether the person is discovering how to make the exercises, and specifically whether he or she is learning practically to make use of the three methods which have been suggested. In this context of experience and not of random contemplation, which runs the risk of being mere intellectual speculation, it is important to see whether the person is really benefiting from the objective content whose light, in faith, becomes a source of experience. In other words, this first evaluation of the quality of the experience as a phenomenon lived by the exercitant allows us already to see to what extent the vision of faith, however intelligent it may be, is limited to the realm of ideas, or whether it is taking hold of the person's concrete life.

Then the true evaluation will become, little by little, that of an actual pervasion of this exercise of presence. For with the passage of time it is possible to discover whether the person's presence in faith stops short on some higher levels of personal existence, or whether it reaches into all the zones of one's being—one's spiritual life, but also one's social, professional, apostolic, emotional, sexual, psychological, communitarian, and political life. Hence it is important to extend the time of the actual experience. In time all of this becomes the subject of evaluation.

To sum up, we must, first of all, see that the person acquires the skill of exercising himself or herself, of becoming present to everything in faith. Secondly, we should verify the degree of the permanence of this presence by making sure that the vision inspired by faith is renewed or deepened. Then it becomes possible to turn our attention together—the retreatant and the director—towards the possible lasting reverberations of this attitude in real life.

3. Some Practical Observations

a. The Foundation and the Viewpoint of Faith

It seems quite evident that the subject matter proper to the Principle and Foundation is, in the experience of the Exercises, strictly that of the total and overall vision of Christian faith. Further, the exercise flowing from it is carried out on the level of a life of faith which becomes clearer and deeper as it tends to penetrate the retreatant's whole concrete life.

From this we must conclude that the Exercises, like the Foundation of them, are meant only for a person who has faith. This faith may be poor and weak, but in the making of the Exercises it will find substantial nourishment which will strengthen and inspire it so as always to be put into practice in a committed Christian life.

A crisis of faith is one of the cases to be detected during the period of preparation, so as to treat it before undertaking the stage of prayer in depth. If this is not done, the person's spiritual balance might be insufficient to carry out the experience of the Exercises effectively. Of course, we have met persons who said they were practically unbelievers or in a serious crisis of faith and yet who drew real profit from the Exercises which they had been encouraged to make. Nothing can be said against this. But if we consider the true experience of the Exercises, which aims at a complete commitment to the following of Christ with full spiritual, evangelical awareness of what this involves, certain basic conditions should be maintained. Among these, the first condition is an attitude of receptivity to further progress in faith. Otherwise one would be condemned to giving the Exercises for thirty days just to prepare persons—on some vague future day, perhaps—to undertake the true experience of the Exercises.

b. The Retreatant's Personal Faith History

Another practical consequence of basing these Exercises on a growing and deepening faith has reference to the personal faith history of the retreatant.

He or she is invited to purify and adjust his own faith vision. In the measure that the life of faith is presented as the interpretation of reality through the light of revelation, he should take the time to rediscover the lines of convergence in the history of his past experience. This will enable him not only to personalize his presence to God's universe still more, but also to create the continuity which this personalization requires. When certain of the essential elements of personal faith are consciously present at the outset, an authentic future of this experience is more likely. The retreatant is thus enabled to grasp the continuity which must exist between what now urges him forward and the faith history which, more or less consciously, has nourished and fortified him until now.

With this in view, it would help, in the beginning, to make a brief inventory of the strong points in the person's spiritual history. These points often become clearer in the light of the overall vision presented in the Principle and Foundation. In this way the personalization of the spiritual experience will be made in a healthier and more conscious manner, and it will be easier to discern in it the action of the Holy Spirit, who ordinarily in the life of the person concerned reveals himself intimately by building in continuity upon the person's past.

c. The Comprehensive Character of the Foundation

We cannot insist too strongly on the comprehensive character to be attributed to the vision of the Principle and Foundation, which corresponds strictly with the vision of biblical faith—and for Ignatius, with the worldview brought to him by the illumination beside the Cardoner. The Christian spiritual experience is essentially universal in its objective content. We must be careful not to narrow down too quickly to the level of the person this totality which can throw so much light on the person's own situation within it. An exaggerated personalism, often degenerating into individualism, and a too hasty asceticism have frequently distorted this vision by enclosing it within the narrow circle of "God and myself."

On the contrary, in the context of the interpretation we have just proposed, it will be understood that a great deal of time must be devoted to the contemplation of the universal—the whole of reality perceived and accepted in the light of faith—so that it may generate a desire truly growing through an interior movement towards a commitment as total as possible. In other words, the overall vision of faith, with the attractive destiny it brings, the beatific vision, is the source of the all-embracing attitude of a "committed presence" in faith. The prolonged personalized contemplation of the universe calls for participation, but participation makes demands of knowledge on the objective level and of conversion on the subjective level which only the rest of the exercise on the Foundation will make clear. At this point the important thing is to have a lively desire for the experience to which corresponds, in germ, the positive attitude of indifference mentioned at the end of the Ignatian text on the First Principle and Foundation. It is a thousand times more important to encourage the contemplation of the content of the vision evoked by the first part of this text—God, man, all created things—than to speculate on the virtues which would spontaneously flow from it and which are dealt with in the second part of the text. Time must be allowed for contemplation to produce its fruit.

d. The Ultimate Criterion for the Verification

Experience teaches us that after the exercitant has sufficiently matured through a series of exercises, the most significant criterion for verifying the quality of her or his "Foundational" experience of faith consists in finding progressively more of the main characteristics of the faith vision set forth in the contemplation. In other words, the question is to see to what extent the truths presented on the objective level in the contemplation are being gradually integrated into the exercitant's outlook and practice, even summarily, in his or her life on the subjective level of experience. Thus we can ascertain that the character of the person who deeply absorbs the spirit of the Foundation opens wider to an overall vision which enlarges his interior horizon. Then he or she spontaneously becomes open to growth, to a transformation, in which the requirements of the Foundation are desired and accepted courageously (here we have a dynamic vision). At the same time, one is caught up in a whole network of vital relationships on both the horizontal and the vertical planes (a personalized outlook toward God and the world). Finally, a stronger unity develops within the person, an efficacious integration takes place, as one more clearly realizes one's own personhood—as one more definitely situates oneself as an "I," fully alive, in God's plan for the universe and for humankind (a unifying vision).

Chapter 4

THE FIRST WEEK:
INTEGRATING THE PROBLEM OF EVIL
INTO THE WORLDVIEW OF CHRISTIAN FAITH

In the general framework we have proposed, the First Week constitutes the second stage in this section I, which makes the viewpoint of faith something more clearly understood and habitually applied to the details of daily life. This new stage aims to show the retreatant the place of the problem of evil in God's plan of creation and thus to make our experience of the vision arising from Christian faith more realistic and more personal.

A. The Objective in This Second Stage

1. Relation between the Foundation and the First Week

The first stage turned the retreatant's attention to the acceptance of a very positive overall vision, that of biblical faith in the God of life, who keeps himself present to the unfolding of creation until it reaches its full achievement in Christ through the Holy Spirit—the Spirit of God "joined to the spirit of the person" for the accomplishment of this unique and universal task. Now, with the Hebrews of the Bible (for example, in the Book of Job) we wish to carry to their conclusions the questions which this overall statement of faith poses. In the very context of their faith in the living and just God, we meet the problem of evil inherent within it.

It is important to tackle this problem in order that our experience may remain realistic and not be frittered away in mere words, and thus deserve the reproach of blithely skipping the most difficult questions of human existence. Another reason, however, plays an even greater role in this matter whose influence will be better seen later on as an even stronger factor. This is the concrete awareness of our collective and individual smallness or spiritual poverty which becomes a real connection point for our experience of salvation. Here the infinite abyss of the eternal, ever-present, unconditional love of God is more existentially perceived. For this is the greatest of all mysteries—that he loved us first, while we were yet sinners (Rom. 5:8).

What we are undertaking then, in this second stage, is a kind of amplification of the Principle and Foundation of the *Exercises*, that is, a repetition extending to its limits the examination of an extremely important point of detail, which becomes the occasion of a vital experience of the positive dynamism of our basic vision, as well as a means of concrete insertion into the mystery of love underlying it. Where sin increased, grace abounded all the more (Rom. 5:20). We, therefore, remain on the universal level, that of the overall vision, but we intensify the application of this light of faith in order to penetrate further into the heart of this living, difficult, concrete reality. Its positive character should emerge strongly beyond the limits of our most intimate radical smallness.

By keeping this perspective in mind, we pursue the precise objective of this First Week. By integrating an understanding of the problem of evil —our own evil—into the dynamic viewpoint arising from our saving faith, we experience the true liberation which Christ our Savior brings us. We cannot in practice today insist too strongly on this point, especially with those persons who are accustomed to the more traditional interpretations of the *Exercises*. Since the primary subject matter of the First Week is evil, sin, and all its consequences (as Ignatius states), it has been customary to make it too exclusively the objective of this stage—to know one's sin, to steep oneself in the thought of sin in order, if possible, to emerge from it purified by the mercy of God. In this way it is very easy to misplace the accent during this Week, as the long-current practice demonstrates very clearly. I should say that meditation on the reality of evil and its meaning is only the occasion for a deeper contemplation to discover and measure the abyss of God's love manifested in Christ our Savior, to whom we must finally surrender ourselves completely if we wish to begin to live.

The real objective of contemplation during the First Week is the history of salvation and of our place, my place, in God's plan. Sin is seen as the attempt to thwart that plan. This history casts much light on the mystery of evil itself, and it carries us beyond these powers of death into the freedom of Christ our Savior. If this fruit of liberation which impels us to follow Christ is not sufficiently developed, the results of the Second Week itself remain largely missed and replaced by a striving for a liberation still unachieved.

Consequently, when St. Ignatius, right from the first exercise places us in the presence of Christ on the cross where the whole of salvation history is summed up,[1] he is using the ongoing light of this history in its direct relation with the expansive viewpoint of faith, and he wants us to consider and ponder the reality of evil from which God in his love comes to deliver us. It will, then, always be in the light of this merciful love of the living God and of Christ our Savior that Ignatius desires us to make these exercises of the First Week. Later I shall discuss a certain ambiguity which must be overcome in practice and which can sometimes lead some persons to begin the contemplation of Christ already in the First Week.

2. *The Problematic and Its Interpretation*

Some considerations regarding the content will now expand what I have proposed as the objective of this second stage of the experience. In fact, it would not be difficult to go immediately to the next step in this stage of experience (that is, to the concrete exercises) and to present the problem of evil in relation to the history of creation, in order to allow the contemplation to make its own way towards a search for interpretation from the faith vision. But I have discovered with time that it is better to tackle the problem outside the subject matter of contemplation, and in more direct and explicit terms. My purpose is to place it more clearly within the vision of faith which itself opens up ways of interpretation. The actual meditations will lead the retreatant to make a personal assimilation of this first reflection. For, with Ignatius, we shall come back in a realistic way to this matter proposed for our contemplation, considered as a living reality existing and evolving in the world created by God.

So it is a clear choice I am making—to explain the meaning of the problem of evil as it is presented and interpreted in faith. Why am I doing this? Because experience has taught me that the retreatant can then, in the light of this faith view which has been explained, contemplate the true reality presented in the Ignatian meditations of the First Week. Otherwise it happens that she or he remains on the surface of these realities (which in fact are difficult to integrate), with the result that this stage of the experience is considerably impoverished. Let us say that a perfect analogy exists between this "didactic" introduction to Ignatius' meditations themselves, which ought to be made in the light of revealed faith which is enhanced by exegetical interpretation for a true contemplation of the gospel mysteries. It should be kept in mind, however, that I place these reflections, communicated to the retreatants, before all the meditations of the First Week and as a continuation of the introduction to this second

---

1   See the colloquy he suggests to the retreatant (*SpEx*, [53]).

stage which we are entering. After all, the objective of this stage is "that which I desire" (*id quod volo*).

Therefore, these complementary reflections consist in proposing the problem of evil in all its complexity, and in drawing out from it the interpretation proposed by the vision of faith on the level of its origin and its conquest. When this integration is not securely based on a biblical foundation, it happens that the retreatant is asked to make an effort to integrate the problem of evil in the vision of foundational faith, but that he or she is left rather with the problem of evil than that of integrating it into its place in his faith view of God, the created universe, and his or her own place in it.

a. The Statement of the Problem

By the word "evil" we are designating here the two species of evil, physical and moral, linked together only on a very precise level—that experienced in connection with our smallness or poverty. In fact, we are dealing with physical evil, without immediate reference to human freedom, and with moral evil, which man can commit within the limits of his freedom; we are dealing with evil suffered and evil committed. The relationship between these two realities must not be placed on the level of any kind of responsibility or culpability, but—as has just been said— on that of a manifestation of our limitations, of our insignificance in comparison with God and the rest of creation; and that on the social and collective level as well as on that of individual persons. The whole of this complex reality is called "evil," very often prescinding from any judgment about responsibility. Whatever be the guilt involved, real or nonexistent, the evil suffered and committed swells up to become that real-life obstacle blocking man's progress. It also delays or interrupts the progress of the world toward the end God had in creating it. This end, in the view of faith, is something very positive: to mirror forth God's attributes to intelligent beings, that they may come to know him and love him and, by freely obeying his directives, merit their way to increased self-fulfillment in the joy of the supernatural beatific vision. Certain of these limitations by their more or less irremediable character—for example, wear and tear, old age and death—constitute a real negation of God's end in creating: more abundant life.

Therefore, in order that the Reign of God may arrive, these limitations must be broken by a "passage" that leaves room for life, beyond the experience of rupture, of wear and tear, and of death, which are their everyday expressions.

b. The Search for an Interpretation

There are at least two levels of interpretation by which we can approach the problem from the viewpoint of faith. One concerns the origin of evil both suffered and committed; the other concerns its conquest in Messianic hope and in the merciful love of Christ.

c. The Origin of Evil in the Interpretation of Christian Faith

As we have seen, the notion of evil is ambiguous. If we take up moral evil, it seems easier to find its origin in ourselves, in a free created being's natural proneness to err. Insofar as we are created, in the process of becoming and not yet fulfilled, we experience limitations on every level. These limitations of themselves are not an evil; they are nonfulfillments called to be fulfilled. But they may become occasions which man takes to abuse the creative order of life. For temptation takes hold of the creative and positive limitations to transform them into something forbidden which frustrates the freedom to grow to fulfillment.[2]

What, then, is the basic meaning of the evil which is sin in the history of humankind? The Bible itself answers this question in a visual fashion in Genesis, chapters 1-3. There we see that, insofar as they are created beings, a man or woman must enter time and submit to the laws of their existence. As free created beings, they can freely accept this state of possible self-development; they can either foster or resist the potentialities which lead to improved life. Sin is the person's refusal to accept the condition of a created being because it is a refusal of the temporality which essentially includes this condition of becoming, a refusal of the time necessary for the fulfillment which would result in the fullness of existence. The desire to succeed immediately, along with fear of the unknown inherent in the lengthy process of becoming, easily takes hold of the fallible creature who is terribly lacking in what future fulfillment promises. The thirst for anticipated fulfillment—"you will be like gods"—transforms into a kind of pseudo-infinity the temporal and perishable present moment which presents itself as easily obtainable. In this case having is substituted for being and becoming: we grab something and take possession of it for ourselves, with the feeling that we are becoming, are fulfilling ourselves —"she saw that the tree was good for food . . . a delight to the eyes and . . . to be desired to make one wise" (Gen. 3:6). This is the root of the evil we commit, cupidity—"for the love of money is the root of all evils"

---

2 On this subject see the reflections of Paul Ricoeur in *Fallible Man: Philosophy of the Will* (Chicago: Henry Regnery Co., 1967).

(1 Tim. 6:10).

In this way moral evil becomes a refusal of fidelity to the creative order of life within us and outside us, in material creation and in our relationship with others. In this sense, it is basically a movement against nature. It runs counter to the development of our very being in its natural orientation towards life—the life which has its own demands if it is to be the genuine life which its Creator intended. Man is neither the author nor the master of that life. To show that is the purpose of the command not to eat from the tree of knowledge of good and of evil, under penalty of becoming subject to death. It also teaches how a complete self-determination can thwart progress toward a better life.

Thus moral evil is also seen as a movement against love, particularly in the insistent revelation through the Prophets. They were trying to make the Hebrews understand that, beyond their fidelity or infidelity to the obligations arising from their agreement to the terms of the Old Covenant, they were literally living a "history of love," a tale of grace and of loving kindness on the part of God, creator and liberator. In Hosea the sin of idolatry is clearly termed adultery. For every sin goes contrary to a movement of love toward which, in the last analysis, we are basically orientated. Love creates life and fosters the development of life, its deepening, and its expression in the fruit of love.

Up to this point we have been tracing the origin of moral evil by starting from the limited and frail structure of the created human being and passing from there to its presence in the history of mankind. What is the case in regard to physical evil such as loss of an arm, of evil which is inflicted upon us? Can we present it simply and merely as a consequence of moral evil, as was done by some when they interpreted chapter three of Genesis literally?

If our answer is yes, then we meet with two serious objections. One comes from the Bible itself which, from Job to Jesus, is opposed to finding the necessary cause of suffering in the guilt of sinful man, or in that of his parents. So we do not find any real solution in the field of inflicted evil when we have recourse to this kind of interpretation. For, as we know, many evils do not depend on our bad will any more than they can be cured by our good will, our state of grace, or our personal holiness: for example, an earthquake, a war which lays waste a whole region, murder committed by a sick and irresponsible person, a simple bad case of flu or of paralysis, or any other natural infirmity.

A second objection comes from the literalistic interpretation which links the existence of suffering to man's introduction of moral evil into the world. This too is refuted by scientific facts. We know that the world could not have passed from a state of perfection (of harmony and immortality) to a new beginning at the moment when sin, moral evil, was introduced into it. The line of evolution from a poorer to a better kind of existence, progressively accomplished, is very clear; and even the biblical account of creation may be easily adapted to these statements, especially since revelation as such is silent regarding any detailed hypotheses in this paleontological field. Before man was created, suffering existed, the various forms of destruction were present in abundance, discord was no less evident in material creation than now, and death put its final touch on everything. Still more, man was created from this same corruptible matter of which the entire cosmos is composed. He, too, was destined to develop, to suffer, and to die if he were left merely to his own nature—that of a created and corruptible being.

On the one hand, then, we should not be naive in our presentation of physical suffering, by placing on man's shoulders more burden of evil than that for which he is responsible. On the other hand, a difficulty remains. In the Bible our vision of faith sees a link between the two realities. In chapter three of Genesis it is explicitly affirmed, in a manner that we can visualize, that human beings committed evil from which many other forms of inflicted evil arose: concupiscence, physical suffering, the burden of toil, barrenness of material creation, death. What are we to say of all this?

We know that these chapters in Genesis do not refer to historical events such as literal interpretation would have us believe; instead, they are proposing a realistic and theological interpretation of the historical reality of evil and its origin. If it is true that moral evil in the world increases suffering, such as the innumerable consequences of culpable hatred or indifference, of divisions, conflicts, and wars, it is equally true that man did not introduce into the world the physical evil (lesser being) linked, as we have seen, to the corruptible condition of all created beings, material and human. But if he did not introduce it—and this is important —by his free action which makes use of creation for selfish ends rather than to further its development in the light of the transitoriness of life, man has condemned the world to remain imprisoned within its limits, within its perishable condition: "You are dust, and to dust you shall return." Henceforth another Person, responsible for creation and accredited by God, must come to live completely his consent to bear time until its fulfillment and thus enable the created universe to achieve the end for which God created it; this Person must do this by means of continual detachment, the necessary condition for all growth. Such will be the obedience of Christ even unto death.

Thus, in our vision of faith, the world is no longer "subject to futility"

(Rom. 8:20).[3] We can still do evil with created things, but we can never snatch them from their long hope, founded in Christ, of a true birth to life. For all this already is and will be, thanks to him who, in his own flesh first of all, broke down the natural limits of the evolution of the world.

d. Our Rising above Evil

The beginning of an answer to the problem of evil is found in the Old Testament; its completion appears in Christ, dead and risen, and placed at the head of all the nations.

We have already said that the Hebrews in their faith faced the problem of inflicted evil, merely suffered, and not directly connected with the guilt of moral evil. In other words, they were content to contrast affirmations of their faith in the God of life against negative realities which they experienced daily: disorder, destruction, suffering, and death. In answer, we can say that they were not content with tracing the origin of evil to the structures of fallible man and to the story of creation in order to reconcile these enigmatic limitations with the hope of life fostered by the experience of the Covenant and of the Messianic promise. They went further than this with the Book of Job, opening the way to the answer which the New Testament was to furnish in the person of Christ, who became the closer-than-expected point of contact with the living, transcendent God.

In the Book of Job, Israel takes up again, in the form of a discourse, the efforts at rational explanations available from this people's own human tradition and from some of the surrounding civilizations. But in the name of that same experience of their limitations when they were asking the questions, and out of honesty before the radical character of these questions posed in a spirit of faith, Job—and Israel through him—refuses these rational explanations which give some mental solace, but fall far short of what we now know from God's revelation. Going right to the limits of their questioning, the Jews gave their answer, a unique one which goes beyond the order of natural reason alone. Their answer to the enigma of evil lies in their experience of God. Chapters 38 through 42 of Job tell us, in literary style and figures which enable us to perceive the matter more concretely, of the interior experience of meeting God, of his present and active preeminence. "O Lord who lovest the living, thy immortal spirit is in all things," the book of Wisdom will state more clearly (chapter 11). This response drawn from lived experience is not necessarily of the order of explanatory reasoning; here, it goes well beyond it. It might be summed up

---

3 On this, see *Biblical Theology and the Spiritual Exercises*, no. 7 on p. 344.

as follows: Evil exists; we constantly experience it; but we have had an experience of the God of life who rises above the potentialities of evil; and we are sure that because of him we are in spite of everything progressing towards life.

This line of confidence in him in whom we trust will become more intense in the light of the Incarnation. It will grow into a fully living hope through the Christ who came among us "with all power in heaven and on earth," and who is risen from the dead and placed at the head of a new world.

At the term of this reflection we can say that physical and moral evil still exists, that it can capture us, that it reveals our radical collective and individual weakness and is so widely diffused that it might cause us to despair. But viewed in the total vision of faith, this reality of evil gives us a truer conception of the length, the breadth, and the depth of the love of God which is expressed in the whole of creation, and especially manifested in Christ and in his Church: God eternally changeless, the love which saves and which is unfailingly present, unconditional, gratuitous, active, personal. It is the experience of God which alone continues to be our only real solution to the enigma of evil, "our evil"; the experience of God, especially when grasped in this undreamed-of closeness to Jesus incarnate and crucified. In the colloquy of his first meditation in the *Exercises*, Ignatius invites us to ask him "how it is that, though he is the Creator, he has stooped to become man, and to pass from eternal life to death here in time?" (*SpEx*, [53]).

3. Our Weakness Balanced by Christian Hope

It is self-evident that the full, precise objective content of the First Week will determine the way in which the experience is pursued on the subjective level. On this plane we find the means to attain the objective of this stage—through the fruit we seek, the grace we pray for.

In view of the integration of the concrete problem of evil into the expansive vision of faith, if we maintain both our weakness and our hope as the two poles of this search, we shall understand that the experience will take place in two stages in which the characteristic thoughts should always interpenetrate one another.

The consideration of reality and of the history of universal and personal evil deepens the awareness of our collective and individual weakness. But, carried out from the viewpoint of faith which poses the problem and then interprets it in the light of revelation, this awareness paves the way for a more existential experience of God's loving and gratuitous plan of salvation and spiritual development. He manifests this love by giving us his son,

Jesus, in order to open to us the only way of salvation, the way of truth which sets us free and gives us eternal life.

If we are faithful in weighing and carrying the burden of this living reality of evil by absorbing it into the comprehensive outlook which springs from faith (the work of the first stage, the Principle and Foundation), in the second stage we will firmly situate the experience of the First Week simultaneously on its two bases. It will consist of a deepening of the awareness of our radical human weakness, and also of an experience of Christian hope founded on the infinite love of God as manifested to us in Christ. That is the love which we offend thoughtlessly, but which is still expressed with the same tenderness and which continues to call us to commit ourselves to a way whose only meaning is life. "Now when they heard this they were cut to the heart, and said to Peter and the rest of the apostles, 'Brethren, what shall we do?'" (Acts 2:37).

B. A Way to the Experience Sought in the First Week

To enable an exercitant to assimilate the material globally explained just above, and to achieve the twofold objective, awareness of our weakness and strong Christian hope, a very simple procedure can be followed in guiding her or his experience. There is practically no need to do anything else except to follow the exercises suggested by Ignatius, taking care to interpret them in the light of the previous considerations drawn from the outlook of faith. Since this subject matter is familiar to those who give the Exercises, I shall limit myself to pointing out how the experience may be guided in terms of the twofold objective in view.

1. The Global History of Evil

The first Ignatian meditation, on the Triple Sin of the angels, Adam, and any individual person, takes up again in its own way the whole history of sin. Ignatius did not intend that three meditations be made, each one concerned with one point separated from the whole. Using the categories customary in his time, he presents the entire subject matter of the meditation in separate points; but these points are exactly those which punctuate a long history of evil which coincides with the history of the first free created beings in God's creation: the angels. The history of sin among the angels is repeated in the history of man, that history of sin which we find in the Bible, and it is again repeated in today's man or woman, who still retains the full freedom of committing evil with its disastrous personal consequences. In itself it matters little whether or not one meditates on the sin of the angels, on that of Adam, or on that of some contemporary person. But in this line which starts with the beginnings of the creation of free spiritual beings, it is well to keep present before one's mind a history that is vast, permanent, present, one in which the reality of evil makes itself keenly felt. All this must be accepted and interpreted in the perspective of faith which reveals its full dimension of hope and of love in Christ.

How can we nourish, over a long period and in daily life, this vision of evil as a universal history? First of all, let us say that we showed one way by example in the foregoing pages, when we tried to formulate the problem and sought its interpretation from our faith. However, there are many and varied ways of tackling or proposing for contemplation the concrete reality of the universal history of evil. Here I shall treat of three ways which I have been able to use according to need—those of the Bible, of history, and of the present day.

The Bible itself opens several ways to this contemplation of evil, of its significance in the vision of faith, and of its being overcome by God. First, there is the history of Israel, which may be seen in an analytical fashion in the historical books and in a synthetic way in certain of the prophets.[4] The Bible shows us some dimensions of this reality in the global point of view which it furnishes in Genesis, chapters 3 to 11, and in the entire Book of Job.[5]

Finally, it reveals a total superiority over evil in the case of Christ our Savior. He showed his power over both our physical and moral limitations by his healing of sickness, forgiveness of sins, exorcisms of devils, and raising of the dead. We have only to look in the Gospels at the attitude of Jesus towards sinners, the poor, the infirm, and in those passages where he reveals to us in a special way the merciful heart of the Father.

Another path to contemplation may be found in the history of the world, read in a spirit of faith and seen from a sufficient height to enable us to grasp those elements which over and over again culminate in the same great catastrophes which ravage creation, divide peoples, and bring death, while man continues interiorly to desire peace, union, love, and life.

Finally, the events of daily life, if reflected on in a spirit of faith, can continually foster the same experience of an awareness of our collective and individual weakness—but, we should remember, in a world which

4   Ez. 16:23; Hosea 1-3; 11ff.; Pss. 78, 105, 106, 107.
5   Excellent Scriptural commentaries are to be found in Stanley, *Modern Scriptural Approach*, chs. 6 and 7 (pp. 57-72), on Gen. 3:1-19; Ez. 28:12-19; and Ps. 130; and in J. Laplace, *Life in the Spirit*, pp. 44-77.

remains entirely and unconditionally the object of the infinite, patient love of God. "Behold, I stand at the door and knock; if anyone hears my voice and opens the door, I will come in to him and eat with him, and he with me" (Apoc. 3:20).

2. One's Personal History of Evil

From considering this universal or global history to which we have made ourselves intimately present, we now go on to consider directly the personal history of our sins, of our limitations, of our weakness and poverty. It is within this great fallible history that our own history unfolds, in solidarity with paths which encompass every form of evil.

The points which are scattered in Ignatius' meditations according to his method should, however, converge toward the same unique activity in the retreatant's intention—to weigh and see, in the light (Ignatius says "by comparing") of the universal unfolding (which includes the rest of creation, the saints and God Himself), how heavy is the burden of this concrete reality, my own personal history of evil. I see that it too has its place and repercussions in that positive history of creation, redemption, and salvation, so as to measure by this the extent of God's love which I see clearly manifested in all things. "A cry of wonder accompanied by surging emotion" (*SpEx*, [60]).

3. The Repetitions

Once these two meditations have been made, Ignatius asks us to repeat both of them together. It is now only a single history that we continue to examine from our faith vision, so as to discover more and more the aspects and signs of this unfailing love of God manifested in Christ, over and beyond all the weaknesses, poverty, insufficiencies which make of the world and of ourselves—and particularly of my own self—the crippled and suffering child whom God, in his loving kindness, continues to carry toward life.

> But now thus says the Lord,
> he who created you, O Jacob,
> he who formed you, O Israel:
> "Fear not, for I have redeemed you;
> I have called you by name, you are mine.
> Because you are precious in my eyes, and honored,
> and I love you. . . .
> Fear not, for I am with you" (Is. 43:1, 4, 5).

The repetitions are the occasion of a prolonged association which allows the spiritual fruit to ripen and deepen in our own intimate experience, before we pass on to a further stage which will, in a large measure, depend on the preceding one. Thus Ignatius does not set a fixed time or the number of repetitions to be made. They will be determined according to the fruit they produce. During the whole period of this First Week, and especially during the repetitions when our mind is not seeking new matter, it happens that we can derive great benefit from certain penitential psalms as well as psalms of supplication.[6]

4. Hell

The maturing of the exercise of the First Week seems to have been achieved sufficiently when we are called upon to respond to that pressing question evoked by love: "Brethren, what should we do?" But before going on to the next stage, Ignatius requires us to make a meditation on hell. It is a serious time of pause, without a repetition properly so called.

This meditation too ought to be situated in the dynamic perspective of the preceding meditations. As I have presented it in my book on the *Exercises*,[7] it constitutes a realistic hypothesis.

In fact, we have just been considering the universal and personal history of evil, from its origins down to our own day, in order to draw spiritual fruit from this: a firm personal commitment to the following of Christ, the only possible Way to fullness of life. On the point of setting out more consciously on this Way, on that in-depth experience which we want to be ours, Ignatius reminds us that the history of evil too will go on in our own life. And if up to a certain point it had an influence in the past, it still retains all its power to influence us in the future. In prayer and in faith Ignatius wishes us to take a look at this future in which evil will still be at work. While it is true that the love of God will never be wanting to us, we always have within us the possibility of cutting ourselves off from it in full liberty. This is the price we must pay for retaining possession of our freedom. And our past, to a certain extent, is witness to the fact that we can misuse that freedom too lightly. So let us be honest with ourselves, and let us have the courage to look squarely at the ultimate result to which this history of evil would lead us if eventually we should fail in fidelity to love, to life. This is the hypothesis which the meditation on hell puts before us. It is a necessary hypothesis, insofar as it is linked to my freedom and to the respect God will always have for it. No one is forced to enter the Kingdom of Heaven.

Hence it is good for us, making use of a renewed terminology which

---

6 Pss. 27, 32, 38, 42-43, 51, 69, 90, 116, 130, 141.
7 *Biblical Theology and the Spiritual Exercises*, pp. 149-150.

does not confuse symbols with reality, to take the time to deepen our knowledge of this possibility which is ever offered to assist us in our fragility. And in our awareness of our Lord's permanent presence to us all along our road, we will become increasingly grateful that "He has shown Himself so loving and merciful to me" (*SpEx*, [71]).

Moreover, situated within the extension of the Principle and Foundation which has us contemplate our path to richer life as something to be pursued in accordance with God's plan of salvation, this meditation may be accompanied by an explicit apostolic dimension, by its bringing in once more in the First Week a liberating meeting with Christ the Savior. This is what Father Michel Ledrus proposes in his *Thèmes*.[8] He writes:

> The thought of damnation and eternal perdition which threatens sinners (Luke 16:27-31)—my sisters and brothers—should, as with St. Paul, never give me rest (1 Cor. 3:15; 9:22; 2 Cor. 7:5; 11:29). It should be enough to make me run to meet suffering in order to relieve it. . . . To meditate effectively on hell is a work of love, far superior to words of love (*SpEx*, [230]).

C. Some Practical Observations

Here a few remarks will merely be an explicitation of points already mentioned. I come back to them intentionally because they sometimes have a practical importance for the achieving of the experience. Other points will touch on some complementary problems which will be treated only briefly.

1. The Transition from the First Principle and Foundation to the First Week

I have noticed in practice that some retreatants are inclined to anticipate entry into the First Week. The reason for this is the following. While considering the overall vision of faith and its positive, all-embracing, and universal content, it happens that their minds spontaneously settle on the question which arises out of the problem of evil—whether it be the objective evil which we have before our eyes or the personal evil which the retreatant experiences within his or her self. This may become a trap and lead to bypassing one of the essential fruits of this stage, especially if concentration on a point of detail is initiated too soon. Sometimes even a director is caught up in this snare, thinking that the time has come to find the answer to a particular very real problem through the experience of the

8 *Ledrus*, meditation 12.

First Week.

But this can be a real danger at this level when contact with the universal, the overall vision of faith, has not lasted long enough, and when the experience from it has not yet sufficiently matured. It is, of course, true that the overall vision includes the fact of evil and that this element must not be overlooked. (This could be a case of daydreaming and then suddenly discovering that sin does exist.) But it is important to allow time for this overall vision of the Foundation to produce its fruit of illumination and motivation before focusing attention on evil—a point of detail, however vast and important it might be in itself. Otherwise we run the risk of answering the problem with reasons, intended and sought as explanations, rather than with an experience integrating evil and going beyond it into the hope of life and a rooting in love.

When the difficulty arises, we must know how to bring the retreatant back to the long and familiar contemplation of the total vision of Christian faith. Often it is even opportune to forestall the difficulty so as to help the person truly to respect the dialectical reasonings of the exercise. However, for the sake of completeness, I must add that, if by chance the experience moves too rapidly into the First Week (sometimes this is seen only in retrospect), it is rather easy to remedy it. Since the integration of evil should be made in the context of the basic vision of faith, the work of the First Week may be continued, but with more accent on the reference to this vision by helping the retreatant place himself always more and more explicitly on the side of faith, on the side of God and of his love, in his or her exercises on the history and the reality of evil. I would even say that there may be cases when the transition may be anticipated if this well-defined background of faith can be more clearly explained by facing the problem of evil from its viewpoint. This is the case with retreatants who are troubled by too lively an awareness of their own evil tendencies, so that they are deprived of the calm necessary to pursue a serene contemplation of "God and of all the things on the face of the earth."

Finally, when making the transition to the First Week, care must be taken with everyone not to put aside the Principle and Foundation. Since this consists in an overall vision on the objective level, it is always within the compass of this vision that we must take our stand and situate the exercise to be made by clarifying with this vision the particular function of each exercise. All the rest of our Christian experience will consist in learning to live while guided by this dynamic and profound totality, human and divine, by way of constant conversion and commitment which depend both on our own continued effort and on the action of the Holy Spirit.

2. The Dynamic Character of the First Week

Here I merely wish to stress again the necessity of presenting the exercises of the First Week in a dynamic perspective. We are concerned with a history, a process of becoming, which we perceive by going back as far as possible in the past history of the world and in our own personal history, in order to turn it towards the future with all the riches of its invitation, but also with its continual inevitable ambiguity during this life.

That is why I have always considered Ignatius' three meditations quite sufficient for this First Week, if they are duly explained. With their repetitions they provide a long consideration of the whole of salvation history, interspersed with the reality of evil which experience helps to envisage with realism.

Regarding other themes for meditation, such as those of judgment and death, which St. Ignatius himself did not judge necessary to include, I shall do no more than refer to what I have said elsewhere.[9]

3. The Place of Christ in the First Week

In this chapter I have already alluded to a frequent occurrence. Some persons, who are attached to certain habits regarding the practice of the Exercises, have difficulty in undertaking the contemplation of Christ, of the saving love of God manifested in Christ, during the First Week. Invited to contemplate this love in the mysteries of Christ which are its expression, they react by feeling a bit guilty for "encroaching on the neighbor's land," that is, on the contemplations of the Second Week.

It is important in this regard to clear up a serious misunderstanding which might hinder the retreatant from surrendering himself to the full liberating strength of the experience of the First Week. This liberation proposed in the First Week should not be sought anywhere else than in Christ; thus it follows that Ignatius' first exercise is made in the light of the history of Christ the Savior on the cross. This is the mystery which must be clearly formulated, sufficiently explained so that it may produce its fruits in face of the deeply explored reality of deadly evil. Liberation can only be achieved at this price. Liberation should be sought as the fruit of the First Week if one wishes the rest of the Exercises to be devoted to a real, total, and radical commitment to the following of Christ.

What is it, then, that distinguishes the First Week from the Second? Retreatants who regularly make the Exercises have often asked me this question. The distinction does not lie essentially in the mystery contem-

---

9 *Biblical Theology and the Spiritual Exercises*, p. 148.

plated, which is one and the same in faith. Rather, it is found in its function which respects the various aims proper to Revelation (which is for man!) and is adapted to the progress of the believer. Before the Gospel can become a practical challenge for a true commitment in the present moment, determined by the movement of the Spirit, it is first of all the Incarnate Word creating life and loosening the bonds with which sin restricts that life. These stages must be experienced, and their path will always substantially be the same—Christ, the only Way and foundation, which no one will ever change.

> For no other foundation can anyone lay than that which is laid, which is Jesus Christ (1 Cor. 3:11).

4. The Result of the First Week

The result of the First Week should without a doubt coincide with the objectives foreseen on the subjective level—with regard to a sharper awareness of our radical smallness and spiritual poverty, both collective and individual. This is the corollary in faith of a more committed experience of Christian hope, of the love of God manifested in Christ, the Liberation of the interior person and the Way of life.

It is, however, possible to discern a little more exactly what is the meaning, for the retreatant making the Exercises, of the experience of this sought-for spiritual fruit. In fact, the person of the First Week who has been making the exercises, for a long time prayerfully contemplating this twofold reality (salvation history and the living reality of evil), will feel himself drawn towards total humility, that is, the absence of any possible interior pretension, as well as toward a complete availability, always based on the unfailing love of God. This person realizes how far "the love of Christ urges" him or her on, and thus offers himself humbly and willingly to live and labor to become the total person that Christ wishes.

When well made, the First Week inspires a total giving (*caritas*) with light and discernment (*discreta*) according to the divine plan. All the dispositions of the Second Week are thus attained at the end of the First Week. Those of the "more" (*magis*) which the meditation on the Kingdom takes for granted have been sufficiently acquired through the foregoing experience.

5. Confession

We know that Ignatius desired the meditation on "personal sins" to be made without reference to confession. In this way he wanted to avoid transforming this dynamic contemplation ("the history") into an examination of conscience, which is rather static in character and inevitably centered on the person himself. On the contrary, he turns it towards that luminous totality in which the retreatant must learn to integrate himself in spite of his smallness.

But once the point of sensitivity to the reality of evil, on the one hand, and a mature experience of hope, on the other, have been reached, confession takes on a new meaning. At the end of the First Week, it can be a direct and immediate manner of expressing the love which becomes, as it were, "urging" at this point in the experience. Now love purifies and unites. It is in keeping with Ignatian practice that this stage end with the sacramental and communal penitential act, reconciling, making reparation, and restoring the most complete communion with Christ and with his living body (*SpEx*, [44]).

It may happen, however, that certain persons put off, until after the election or during the meditation on the Passion, the special confession which rather frequently accompanies the experience of the full Exercises. These two high points certainly offer a similar interest in view of the compelling love which is then experienced. It is in love, and as a response to love, that the desire for purification should be experienced—an ever greater purification in order to attain a more complete union with the Body of Christ.

Concerning the person to whom the retreat confession should be made, St. Ignatius' remark is always valid—it is not at all necessary that confession be made to the director of the Exercises.[10]

---

10 According to St. Ignatius it would even be preferable that the confession should not be made to the person giving the Exercises (see *SpEx*MHSJ, p. 779). This opinion was repeated by Polanco (ibid., p. 810), the *Directorium Granatense* (p. 957), the *Breve Directorium* (p. 981), and the Directories of 1591 and 1599 (pp. 1043 and 1145).

THE SECOND WEEK:
THE KINGDOM
AND THE DEEPENING OF ONE'S SPIRITUAL LIFE

For the contemplation of the Kingdom and the interpretation of it, I shall closely follow chapter 5 of my book *Biblical Theology and the Spiritual Exercises*.[1] However, several introductory aspects will be slightly modified, especially because of the context in which the experience "made in daily life" is situated. In this case we are ordinarily accompanying persons who have been more carefully prepared, in accordance with the demands of the "more" or "greater" (*magis*) which St. Ignatius develops more fully at the beginning of this stage.

A. The Place and Objective of the Meditation on the Kingdom

1. The Connection with Ignatius' Worldview

According to Ignatius, the spirit of the *magis* dominates the beginning of this stage which leads, in the experience of the "full Exercises," to a more definitive commitment. According to him it could very well happen that the Exercises would have to be discontinued after the First Week. The reason for this is that the complete Exercises were truly reserved for those whom he judged capable of a more total commitment of their Christian life to the following of Christ.

I have already spoken of these basic dispositions when I dealt with the preparation for the Exercises in chapter 2. In our present-day context, when culture is more accessible and more widespread and faith is much more seriously questioned by secular life, I feel that these basic dispositions have become those of every tested Christian life. Today as soon as faith tends to become more conscious and committed, it is practically brought face to face with the radicality of the Gospel which excludes all mediocrity.

---

1   *Biblical Theology and the Spiritual Exercises*, pp. 166-213.

That is why the problem of basic dispositions is aptly placed at the beginning during the preparatory stage of the Exercises made in daily life, just as it was for Ignatius.

But in addition to making sure of these general dispositions, we think it is expedient here to insist, as Ignatius did, on the quality of the fruit of the First Week, since this gives a practical initiation into the second stage of the Exercises with the rigor and the radicality of the Gospel. As we have seen, this fruit is above all a fruit of liberation—liberation from oneself, from one's limitations, from the evil which marks us. It allows us to surrender ourselves more completely to the grace of Christ the Savior and to the total commitment which calls us to follow him. In order that the experience may fully become a listening and a commitment to the following of Christ, his truth must have worked in us this first radical liberation which surrenders us completely to the action of grace and to the influence of the Spirit.[2] The retreatant will then have no other desire but to answer the Lord, to discern his calls and, through them, the will of the Father. It is a new, but always the same, road which opens out before him, and he cannot but respond, "What ought I to do for Christ?"

So in the spirit of the authentic *magis*, rediscovered in this very person of the retreatant, we can begin the meditation on the Kingdom by situating it more directly within the context in which the experience has progressed until now.

2. In the Context of One's Own Life

In our context, this meditation will be much more than an introduction to the contemplation of the Gospel events of the Weeks that follow. Or rather, it will fill this role insofar as it truly completes the preceding stage by formulating the overall vision of faith more explicitly and by leading it on to the next stage—that of "assimilation," which is its direct consequence and where the experience takes on quite a different rhythm of evolution.

I have had occasion in other contexts to accompany the spiritual experience of persons who did not refer to the Exercises of Ignatius, to his series of very original meditations. Now, I have noticed that the passage from the stage of explicit formulation of faith vision on the universal level to that of assimilating in detail the mysteries of Christ gave rise to a certain difficulty—there was a definite rupture in the rhythm of the

---

2   The classical case of Pierre Favre comes to mind. Ignatius gave him the First Week of the Exercises but made him wait more than four years before allowing him to make the complete Exercises.

experience.

Yet the experience of the two preceding stages (the overall vision of faith and the integration of the problem of evil) culminated quite normally in this affirmation of Christ our Savior who calls us to follow him in hope and in love. So it seems fitting that by prolonging the stage of explicit formulation of faith vision through a consideration such as that of the Kingdom, the experience of what is universal emerges into the multiple details of the Gospels which, so to speak, it evokes more consciously.

3. The Precise Objective of This Meditation

The precise object of this meditation, then, will be, in continuity with the two preceding stages involving a more explicit formulation of the overall vision, to reach the very heart of this vision of faith, in which Christ has a unique role in the achievement of the Kingdom. On this same level of explicitation and deepening, we must have a clearer, more comprehensive awareness of this great event—from the point of view both of its significance (that is, Christ's mission) and of the reverberations it produces in the concrete lives of men and women (their fervent participation in the life of faith), and in the subsequent personal experience of the retreatant.

In this sense, the meditation on the Kingdom will make the person of our Lord, who establishes the Kingdom, the explicit foundation for all the subsequent contemplations. They will enable us to appropriate the saving aspect of Christ in the hidden life, to hear his proclamation of the Kingdom in the public life, and to participate in his saving action, the paschal mystery, which completes the Father's plan of creation. "For no other foundation can anyone lay than that which is laid, which is Jesus Christ" (1 Cor. 3:11).

To sum up, the one making the Exercises completes, in this fairly short time given to the contemplation of the Kingdom, the explicit formulation of the vision of Christian faith, of its comprehensive character, and of its principal points of contact—the progressive history of salvation, across the living reality of evil, being completed by and in Christ. But being thus centered on Christ who achieves the Kingdom and who calls us to follow him, the same contemplation turns us towards the future. It introduces us to the assimilation of the mysteries of Christ and draws us on along the only road for us to take, the one revealed to us especially in the privileged setting of the Gospel, which is the light of life for that spiritual experience made "according to the way of Jesus."

B. The Structure of the Ignatian Meditation

1. A Double Principle of Discernment

The meditation on the Kingdom establishes a link between the end of the First Week and the beginning of the Second. This link has to do with the discernment required for the ordering of love in the retreatant's experience. The aim of the meditation on the Kingdom is not to arouse generosity; that has already been acquired as the fruit of the previous stage, which consists in the surrender of self to saving love. Love calls forth love, which then feels a need to express itself in action—to commit itself. Consequently, the remainder of the Exercises presents an experience in discernment of love ("discreet charity"). On the level of the overall faith vision and at the starting point, the meditation on the Kingdom gives us two principles; and the Weeks which follow will make these principles more explicit on both the objective and the subjective levels.

The first principle (and the objective) which will help love to become rightly ordered is Christ himself. The experience of love in the First Week has incited the retreatant to choose the unique way which leads to life: Christ, who brings to fulfillment the plan of God and of our own existence. To examine God's plan of salvation, the "mystery of Christ" in its fullness, is to project its light on the way we choose to follow him. Here we have, on this level, a direct introduction to the contemplation of the mysteries or events of Christ's life which will root the whole experience of discernment in the Truth.

A second principle of discernment proposed by the meditation on the Kingdom concerns the person of the retreatant—his or her history, personality, previous experiences, and present situation. More than ever, the authenticity of the experience obliges us to respect this subjective pole. The discernment which leads to the ordering of love will be carried out only on this condition. We shall see that Ignatius refers us, in a general way, to this element of light and truth by means of his own explanation of his "Parable"; and the rest of the experience will explore this way of discernment through the prolonged process of the election under the personalized movement of the Holy Spirit.

2. The Distribution of the Material

The meditation on the Kingdom may be divided into three parts: (1) the Ignatian parable serving as an introductory exercise which, on the subjective level, disposes the retreatant in a realistic way to heed the call inherent in the proclamation of Christ's mission; (2) the discourse of the Eternal King, which on the one hand clarifies the significance of Christ's intervention in establishing the Kingdom, that is, his universal, priestly, and sacrificial mission; and on the other hand throws light on the baptismal vocation of the Christian as acceptance of salvation in Christ, as well as a sharing in his universal mission and a response to his personal call; (3) finally, the offering of self formulates this response on two levels—that of total commitment to the building of the Kingdom and that of pursuing the spiritual experience immediately ahead. This is a twofold way, of love and of discernment; in other words, a way of charity and of discretion.

In my opinion all the aspects of this meditation should be kept in mind; and it is important to bring out their functioning in the way the matter is presented, so that the retreatant's activity may be directed correctly.

C. The Content of This Exercise in Practice

In order to center the retreatant's attention on what is essential in the vast subject matter of this exercise, I personally follow a different order in the distribution of the material.

First I present what is at the heart of this meditation, that is, the Kingdom and its meaning, the central role of Christ in it, and our sharing in his saving mission; in other words, a brief theology of salvation. Next I point out the ways of offering suggested to each one in a global way, and with Ignatius I insist that we should first keep to the overall aspect, to what is universal, while at the same time explaining the first consequences necessary for the continuation of the experience. Finally I introduce the person to this activity of contemplation and self-offering by proposing the Ignatian parable, applied to the retreatant's own self, as a previous work of preparation which is personal and realistic.

I shall keep to this order in the section which follows, where I present the content of the meditation as I do in practice during "open" and "closed" Exercises.

1. The Mission of Christ

Undoubtedly there are several ways of summarizing and presenting a brief theology of salvation in relation to the mission of Christ and the participation of the Christian in it. For my part, aiming at an experience of clarification, I usually put special emphasis on certain important characteristics of Christ's saving mission.

Everything depends, first of all, on the nature of salvation which the Covenant with the Living God reveals as the final term of human existence —salvation for eternal life. It is then important that the one who accomplishes this universal Pasch for the benefit of a sinful world have the power to accomplish a total reconciliation and to impart a divine life. This is stating in a few words the priestly character of the saving mission of Christ.[3]

Since this mission is accomplished from within—that is, by taking on perishable human nature—it was also necessary that Christ should be "made like his brethren in every respect, so that he might become a merciful and faithful high priest in the service of God, to make expiation for the sins of the people" (Heb. 2:17). This suffices to reveal the sacrificial character of this mission, in which suffering and death constitute the matter of the supreme act of expiation. But this sacred character follows from the fact that these same negative elements of human experience are transformed, made sacred (*sacrum fieri*) by way of expiation and of efficacious "passage" toward life, and as a means of expressing the praise of thanksgiving which Christ renders to the Father together with the whole of creation.

Finally, Christ carries out his mission in the name of the whole universe, at whose head he has been placed as the Messiah; and in this very accomplishment he receives the power to transmit reconciliation and life to every creature on earth and in heaven. He carries the whole of creation along the way he opens up, and he incorporates it progressively into himself by various modes of participation. This is his universal mission, at one and the same time royal and prophetic, which inaugurates the new creation and which will be brought to its fulfillment by the free participation of the "sons of God."

Such is the Kingdom which Christ establishes with the very stuff of creation of which we are a part, redeeming us "by blood and the cross" (Col. 1:20) and actively uniting us to the ascent of the universe in the Spirit toward the Father.

2. Our Participation in Christ's Mission

It is impossible to accept the salvation which Christ offers us if we act only in a selfish and individualistic way. The salvation that Christ offers us is the story of a mission which prolongs and fulfills, in him, the natural history of the whole of creation. Hence, we participate in Christ's salvation to the extent of our participation in his mission, of our active incorporation in this total Body which he is building up, he, the Word of God, become a part of creation.[4]

---

3 For further details see *Biblical Theology and the Spiritual Exercises*, pp. 188-192.
4 See ibid., pp. 192-195.

Our participation also becomes directly enlightened by the saving mission of Christ. Without our realizing it, this participation is a life-giving power which extends the true life of Christ into time and space through our baptismal consecration to be part of a priestly people. It passes through the same sacred way which transforms in turn our actual life and our death into a passage towards life and a praise rendered to the glory of the Father. Finally, it calls every being to be part of God's unique world, his Kingdom, where we are not only priests of this life, but also missionaries and prophets of its universal accomplishment.

> Therefore, if any one is in Christ, he is a new creation; the old has passed away, behold, the new has come. All this is from God, who through Christ reconciled us to himself and gave us the ministry of reconciliation; that is, in Christ God was reconciling the world to himself, not counting their trespasses against them, and entrusting to us the message of reconciliation. So we are ambassadors for Christ, God making his appeal through us. We beseech you on behalf of Christ, be reconciled to God. For our sake he made him to be sin who knew no sin, so that in him we might become the righteousness of God (2 Cor. 5:17-21).

Such is the extent of the Christian vocation on which the mission of Christ throws light, along the line of a Kingdom whose fulfillment is realized in faith and communion. Christian existence, by its very nature— that is, insofar as it is Christian and grafted on to Christ the Savior—is essentially an apostolic existence. To become aware of this fact at this stage is to accept with fuller lucidity the call Christ addresses to us by our baptismal communion with his universal mission of salvation.

3. The Oblation: Total and Radical

St. Ignatius proposes two levels of offering at this point of the experience. At first sight the difference between the two expressions is fairly clear—one has a universal character; the other expresses a more concrete commitment.[5]

Practical experience in this matter has taught me to situate within the context of this stage the two levels we are dealing with. The first one has reference to the task as a whole, perceived more clearly and accepted in its totality. Ignatius also insists that the offering be made in terms of this "task or mission of Christ" and of its significance for us—our Christian vocation. This perspective coincides completely with the aim of this stage of universality, as it is described above.

The second response ought to be well understood so as not to deviate

---

5   See ibid., pp. 197-204.

from the line followed until now, and thus cause certain less happy consequences in the retreatant's experience. For example, it sometimes happens that stages are skipped without one's realizing it. In fact, this more precise offering aims at a certain realism by making clear the possible demands of the commitment. These demands, in their expression, sometimes trouble the desire to be faithful to the experience at the point it has reached.

Yet the examples given by Ignatius (poverty, sickness, short life, and the like) are not what matter here, so they should not be insisted upon. What is important is the decisive, radical aspect which the overall offering takes on by seeking immediately the conditions of realizing it by means of the experience still to come. Hence, the second offering is made in continuity with the first, which is already universal and total and, in line with the experience, to be continued immediately. Thus, it assumes, on the objective level, the character of a serious examination of the very demands of the Kingdom and, on the subjective level, the conditions for its realization in our own personal history.

In other words, based on the total character of the first offering, the second one clearly entails the immediate continuation of the experience of the Exercises, rather than the uncertain future of life. It does so with evangelical realism. Hence, it is the general offering resulting from the Principle and Foundation which is determined here more precisely for every committed Christian and every retreatant who has the spirit of the "more": by seriously choosing to embrace the way of the Gospel. However, it is only at the election that this evangelical offering will assume a precise name in the personal life of the retreatant.

4. The Ignatian Parable

Since I have developed Ignatius' parable at length elsewhere, I shall not here dwell on its meaning or on the manner of applying it to the retreatant's life.[6]

To sum up, let us say that in my opinion Ignatius' parable should not be presented in its old-fashioned wording, nor should it be simply transcribed into more modern terms. The parable has, on the subjective level, a very precise function at the outset of this stage of a more conscious commitment to the following of Christ: It is a means of bringing the Kingdom to fulfillment. It serves to mobilize all the energies of the person which usually find expression on different levels: passions, desires, appetites, aspirations, ambitions. It is by making use of what constitutes one's actual

---

6 See ibid., pp. 177-184.

psychological, spiritual, and social person that the retreatant begins to listen to the Lord and is disposed to follow him with the realism of one's whole personality. In this sense, each retreatant is invited to design his or her own parable, the parable of his or her past life, as it was in history and as he continues to build upon it now. It renders the retreatant present, concretely, to the truth of his or her being. For it is to this totality of one's person that the Lord speaks; this is what He challenges. With his or her whole being the retreatant is now disposed to hear and answer with the greatest possible attention.

D. The Exercitant's Task

In conclusion to all the foregoing, once we have explained this vast subject of Christ as the center and fulfillment of the vision of Christian faith, the retreatant enters on a task which is very simple: He or she creates his parable, the parable of his own life—the aims he pursues, the values he esteems, and so on, in order to be totally present to the remainder of the experience which is progressing along a way becoming ever more personalized. Then he resumes the proposed reflection on the meaning of Christian existence clarified by that of Christ, and already accepted by accepting him, in order to perceive its principal implications and to dispose himself to respond by a more conscious commitment. In doing so he has already reached the stage of the oblation which he will develop still further in prayer—his offering of self for the Kingdom of Christ, and for the immediate continuation of the experience.

When the Exercises are made in everyday life, this meditation usually lasts two or three weeks. As it is an exercise which is still on the level of the universal or general, care must be taken not to prolong it indefinitely. All the rest of the Exercises will take up again, in great detail, on both the objective and subjective levels, the subject matter of this meditation.

As a help to theological reflection on the "universal mystery" of Christ and the meaning of Christian existence, and especially as nourishment for prayer during this period of the Exercises, the retreatant may refer to the following texts:

In *Biblical Theology and the Spiritual Exercises*, the Scripture texts giving a global survey of God's plan, pages 342-344.

Old Testament: Ezekiel 36:16-38; Psalms 2 and 23; Isaiah 49:6.

New Testament: Luke 4:16-22; 9:18-22; 10:1-24; John 7:37-38; 10:1-18; Romans 5:5-19; 2 Corinthians 5:17-21; Colossians 1:15-20 (and parallel passages); Hebrews 1:1-9; 8:6-13; 9:1-22; 1 Peter 2:9-10.

Also Stanley, *Modern Scriptural Approach*, chapter 8 (pp. 78-84), treating of the Messianic entry of Jesus into Jerusalem and into the Temple (Matt. 21:1-17); Laplace, "The Call of Jesus," *Life in the Spirit*, pp. 79-92; and C. A. Bernard, "La participation au mystère du Christ," *IV Corso*, lesson 21.

Chapter 6

CHRIST AND HIS SAVING MISSION:
HIS INFANCY AND HIDDEN LIFE AS A PRELUDE

We are now beginning what I called, in Figure 2 of chapter 2 above, section II of the experience of the Exercises. It differs from section I in several respects: in its content, taken directly from the Gospels; in the semantic problems it raises (exegesis and contemplation); and in the rhythm which it requires (assimilation of the details of the mysteries of Christ). Hence, I shall first propose two series of reflections bearing on our coming chapters 7, 8, and 9 taken as a whole. These are an introduction to this stage of the experience, called one of "assimilation," and an examination of the problem which concerns scriptural exegesis in relation to the exercitant's contemplation. After that I shall take up directly the infancy narratives in the first two chapters of Matthew and Luke, that is, the hidden life of Jesus. These contemplations comprise the first stage in section II.

A. Introduction to Section II of the Retreat Experience: Assimilation

1. A Change of Key

It may appear arbitrary to insist here on the passage from one stage to another in an experience in which the steps follow so naturally one after the other, in a continuity which has stood the test of time. What guides me is the desire to go beyond the bland and rather mediocre effects of some persons' experiences of the Exercises, so as to penetrate more deeply into their internal dynamic, which has nothing to do with half measures. In one sense, my practical experience has made me desire to work out in some detail the implications of this change of key, a change which concerns not only the content of the Exercises but also the method to be used to make the exercise well. It sometimes happens that persons who are more or less analytic have difficulty in adapting to the change of character required by the experience which is about to follow. This difference has led me to introduce the retreatant more consciously to this "new" form of presence to the subject matter proposed in the exercise.

The foregoing observation proceeds from the fact that some persons find the practice of the Exercises in the First Week easier than those which follow. From this point of view the meditation on the Kingdom is in itself a bird's-eye-view meditation on Christ, similar to those in the Principle and Foundation and in the First Week. For others the opposite is true. I should not be surprised if this was the distinction St. Ignatius established among his companions, considering some of them more capable of giving the Exercises of the First Week, and others, of conducting the complete Exercises. I believe that, as far as the accessibility and truth of the Christian experience is concerned, this distinction is connected with a change of musical key, a passage from one stage and kind of explicitation to another, namely, an assimilation which goes far more into details: from a stage of universalized considerations to those which are particularized. In my opinion, this can be overcome both by the one who makes the Exercises and by the one who gives them, through an awareness of the change which helps mentalities to adapt in a more vital manner. What is needed is to discover the ways of proceeding proper for each of us, with our own thought patterns and ways of assimilating.

In the experience of the Exercises until now, the retreatant had to open his or her mind to general perspectives. Even in what concerned evil and Christ, these realities were considered in their relationship to a whole (as an obstacle or a rupture in the case of evil, and in the case of Christ as a way of realization). In each case the totality remained as an explicit point of reference throughout the meditation.

Without ever leaving aside this comprehensive view of a whole which contains every mystery, every reality to be contemplated, it is really to very particular details that we turn our attention now as we begin the Second Week. It may happen that the relationship to the whole is contained in the mystery taken up, for example, in the contemplation on the Incarnation (the hidden life) or in those contemplations concerned with the messianic mission of Christ or the wedding feast at Cana (the public life). All of these take on a universal character through their relation to the "fullness of time." In other mysteries that are contemplated, however, there is less obvious evidence of their connection with this totality; but the retreatant ought to continue to find how to assimilate the totality through the multiple details in which it is enfleshed. Hence, it is good to perceive this precise point clearly, right at the outset in this stage: the key or tone of the experience is going to be modified.

However, let us add that the retreatant who has taken the time really to live the previous stages, and to experience them while respecting their dynamic thrust, can undertake this period of assimilation without too great a risk of getting lost in the multiplicity of details and of having the impression of abandoning the overall vision which has moved him until now. If well guided, he or she will adapt spontaneously to the requirements of this stage. The more one desires truly to live by this totality, the more careful one is to take possession of it.

2. The Three Stages of This Experience

In concluding this introduction, I should like to point out, as I do in directing the Exercises, that this period of assimilation (section II), which aims at one's appropriating the worldview which had been clarified and deepened in the previous stages of the experience, will develop in three stages. They are determined by the very finality of the Gospel revelation which constitutes their primary nourishment. These classical divisions in the message of Christ were introduced neither by Ignatius nor by the tradition of so-called "lives of Jesus." The proclamation of the gospel, under the movement of the Spirit, has made provision for them since the time of the primitive Church. We shall take our inspiration directly from them in our spiritual endeavor.

Each of these stages corresponds to a precise subject matter; and, as a consequence of the function of each subject in revelation, a different object is proposed for assimilation. In other words, under the influence of the message, the assimilation itself takes a different significance which progresses from one stage to the other.

To the Gospel narratives of the infancy, whose deep meaning has to do with the revelation of Christ as the Savior, there corresponds a more spontaneous contemplation which matures one's knowledge of the Lord and intensifies one's desire for a deep union, a "becoming one with Him." This is the first stage. A certain interpretation of the public life, which extends from the Baptism in the Jordan to the Last Supper exclusively, invites the acceptance of the word officially proclaimed in time, addressed to all in faith, and totally personalized by the action of the Spirit who always accompanies the living word. This is the second stage. Finally, from the Last Supper in the Gospels to the Church (the mission) in Acts, Christ carries out a personal, universal, and permanent action; and we can share in it by our consent to offer our entire selves. This is the third period, that of the "paschal mystery," our association with Christ in his suffering, death, and resurrection. This is the heart and summit of the Christian experience. Its actualization will always require the entire cycle of the procedure we have analyzed.

B. A Basic Problem in the Contemplation of the Gospel Mysteries in the Second Week

The place of the Gospel mysteries in the whole of revelation determines their particular function in the Christian experience in general, and in that of the Second Week in particular. In the light of this fact we are better able to organize our necessary recourse to a scriptural exegesis which ferrets out the exact interpretation of the texts. This improves both the presentation of the mysteries and the contemplation of them.

1. The Purpose of the Gospel Events in God's Revelation, in the Experience of Living the Spiritual Life, and in the Second Week

We know that the Gospels are not history in the strict sense of this term, that their authors had no intention of writing their "memoirs." The aim of the Gospels is catechetical. Through the various events which they recount, especially the preeminent event of salvation in Christ, they announce a message of life and propose the teaching which flows from it.

In its catechetical aspect, the Gospel message is aimed directly at commitment to following Christ, for those to whom it is addressed. Thus, the Gospel directly enlightens and nourishes the faith experience of those who willingly accept Christ and his Kingdom. "I came that they may have life, and have it abundantly" (John 10:10).

The pedagogical aim of the Exercises, too, is to help the believer to live the basic Christian experience with greater awareness. At the point at which the Exercises have arrived, the four Gospels are the source from which the retreatant will draw inspiration, as he or she comes into contact with the inspirational revealed mysteries. This is the following of Christ, the *sequela Christi*, under the aspect of communion with Christ's saving role which includes our own human spiritual development, by conforming it to that of the Kingdom moving always towards eternal life.

2. A Problem of Exegesis and Contemplation

By means of contemplation, which is presence in faith, the retreatant welcomes the content of the revealed mystery, in order to learn to communicate in depth with the reality it proffers. In this context it is of the greatest importance to reach the real content of the revelation, and hence of the genuine Christ of revelation, the true Kingdom of revelation.

By means of its complex critical apparatus, exegesis aims at the exact interpretation of scripture texts. It would, therefore, be presumptuous to overlook it when one wishes to propose "the solid and true foundation" of revealed reality, as Ignatius rightly required. Today this science has made great strides which are part of the common patrimony of the life of the Church and of the faith experience of the faithful.

It follows from this that when the mysteries of the Second Week are presented, we must first avoid the mistake of stopping short at a literal sense of the Gospel texts; if by omitting interpretation we think that we shall avoid "errors" of interpretation, we run the risk of exposing the retreatant to an impoverished, if not false, encounter with the Christ of the Gospels.

What is needed is to know how to present the true meaning of revelation through the human intermediary of a language, a text, a culture, and a personality—and in this we are helped by an exegesis which must be of good quality. It is indispensable.

In practice I use the first "prelude" of the Ignatian contemplations, precisely intended to discover this solid and true foundation of the revealed facts. Since this prelude is not the contemplation itself, it can be explained, with the help of exegetical proofs when necessary, to make as clear as possible the true meaning of the mysteries proposed for the exercitant's contemplation. Then the retreatant will take up briefly this initial reflection in order to graft onto it his or her personal activity of contemplation. Thus, once the prelude has been stated, the director has nothing more to do. It is entirely up to the exercitant to explore directly through contemplation (seeing, hearing, tasting, and the like) the concrete mystery or event received right from the start with its true meaning—that which corresponds as closely as possible to the inspiration and revelation which exegesis must clarify.

For further details on these subjects, treated at greater length but from the same perspective, see my book previously quoted.[1]

C. The Infancy and Hidden Life in the Second Week

Here we shall limit ourselves to applying to the first two chapters of Matthew and Luke the principles stated in the preceding paragraph about the objectives common to the Gospel revelation, to the experience of Christian faith, and to the development of the Exercises.

---

1 *Biblical Theology and the Spiritual Exercises*, pp. 219-249 and 270-277. Also lesson 25 of *IV Corso Internazionale per Direttori degli Esercizi*; and Daniel-Rops, *Daily Life in the Time of Jesus.*

1. The Purpose of the Narratives in Matthew 1-2 and Luke 1-2

In the primitive Church the proclamation of the "good news" of salvation corresponded with what is now called "the public life." Peter himself in the Acts of the Apostles (1:21-22), seeking for a successor for Judas in the apostolic college, states that someone should be chosen who has been a witness along with them "during all the time that the Lord Jesus went in and out among us, beginning from the baptism of John until the day when he was taken up from us."

Later on, Matthew and Luke added what has become the introduction to their written Gospels, the narratives of the infancy and of the hidden life. Their aim was to rediscover the roots of this message of life in the very being of Christ, and in this way to make us see that, as soon as he is in our midst and through what he is, Christ is already the life given to men and women. He is eternal life which has come into our perishable world, that is, the fulfillment of the promises.

Luke and Matthew attain this aim, not by explicit discursive or dogmatic statements, as I have just done. Their more Oriental and pictorial expression is that of the Bible, which often has recourse to an image or a concrete narrative to express realities which are sometimes entirely interior, spiritual, even mystical. In the present case Matthew and Luke make use of the midrash, a literary genre which enables them to announce their message (which is doctrinal and not historical) by means of a concrete reflection developed out of a minimum of historical facts (at the very least the fact of the birth of Jesus), by taking matter from earlier scriptural passages. Through a vivid application of these passages to present events, they proclaim the fulfillment of the promises in the very person of Christ. Before he spoke and acted, Jesus made real in himself these promises which in Israel concretize the long march of the whole of creation towards a life which will culminate in Him who is "the life." Within this context the infancy narratives serve to deepen the vital meaning of the overall mystery of the Incarnation, before the Gospels take up the later events in the following of the Word Incarnate.

2. The Purpose on the Objective and Subjective Levels during the Second Week

Why, then, do we contemplate the mysteries of the infancy and the hidden life during the Second Week? The objective clarification which shows us their proper function in the forward march of revelation answers our question, if we wish to respect this revelation which exists for the experience of the believer. The concrete episodes selected by Luke and Matthew enable the person who opens himself to them through faith and contemplation to meet Christ the Savior, the fulfillment of human hopes and of the Kingdom of God. By following the evangelists we are called to meet, beneath the surface appearances, this unique Person who later will offer himself to us as the fulfillment of our own being. Thus, in proportion to the intensity of this attractive discovery—interior knowledge and desire for union, on the subjective level—we shall be more completely attentive to the Living Word when he proclaims himself officially during his public life.

D. The Selection and Distribution of the Subject Matter

It is important, right at the start, to be faithful to the principle just presented. It requires us constantly to relate the particular Gospel events we contemplate to the whole divine plan of salvation through Christ, who realized the reign of God and made possible our own human fulfillment in the beatific vision. In this way we help persons of differing character to order their lives in accordance with the dynamic progress of revelation and its development in function of the Kingdom and of Christ, the life. That is why I shall follow Ignatius' suggestion to begin the contemplation on the infancy by the comprehensive vision proposed in the contemplation on the Incarnation. Then I shall regroup the possibilities of contemplation, not according to a chronological order as Ignatius might have been spontaneously inclined to do in his era (even though he knew very well how to escape from it in a very significant way on occasion); but I shall start from the viewpoints proper to the Gospels of Matthew and Luke. Finally, I shall end with a theological treatment of the hidden life, to which I attribute a special importance, especially for the Exercises made in everyday life.

1. The Introductory Contemplation on the Incarnation

Here I can only recommend Ignatius' suggestion to begin the series of contemplations on the infancy with that of the Incarnation. His way corresponds not only with the chronological order, but he was able to link it with a vision of the whole, on which he insists in his first prelude ([102]), and which is similar to the Prologue of John. It extends from the eternal preexistence of the Word to his historic entrance into this world. But the vision is vast, going beyond the point of time chosen for the Incarnation itself and connected with the multiplicity of places and situations included in the event. Christ enters into this totality, beyond that point of entrance in time and space concretized by Nazareth, Mary, and the angel of the Annunciation ([101-109]).

75

The advantages of adopting this point of departure are the following. It situates the mystery within the whole of revelation and its significance for the benefit of human beings. It links the contemplation of the facts with Christ, the Eternal Lord of the Kingdom, and reveals him as the beginning of the Way into it. It is a good orientation for the particular mysteries that follow, like the Annunciation and the Nativity, which then become for the exercitant clearer visualizations, in the language of images and events, of the unique great mystery of the Incarnation: God with us and establishing in us and in creation his Kingdom of life, the mystery of greatness and power, of salvation and life, realized through stripping, weakness, and vulnerability, a stumbling block for some, but for all, the fulfillment of time and the summit of history.

2. Matthew 1-2 and Luke 1-2

Matthew retains four incidents of the infancy and shows its significance as the summit of all history by combining citations from the Old Testament in the literary form of the midrash. With one stroke he links the genealogy of Jesus to the virginal conception of Mary and to the "official" insertion of the Child within the human lineage of David through the intermediary of Joseph. Then comes the adoration of the Kings, which reveals to the Jews the universal character of the Kingdom inaugurated by the coming of Jesus. Finally, as a sign of contradiction, the Lord's presence already entails the concerted persecution which culminates in the rejection of Christ and in the sacrifice of the holy innocents who suffer violence for the sake of the Kingdom of God.

On the other hand Luke, instead of citations (such as those of Matthew in his use of the midrash), makes use of the literary structures of Daniel (8:16-19; 9:20-27) and Malachi (3:1). By the construction of his narrative, he reveals that the mere coming of Christ among us, preceded by that of John (in regard to both annunciation and birth), fulfills the period of seventy weeks of years announced in Daniel. Malachi had stated (3:1): "Lo, I am sending my messenger. . . . And suddenly there will come to the temple the Lord whom you seek, and the messenger whom you desire." By the coming into the temple (but here in the form of the ritual presentation) of the infant Christ whom Simeon saw and interpreted, we have the fulfillment of the ages in Jesus. Life has come into this perishable world. This is the great "good news" to be announced to all, which is already welcomed joyfully by those who are poor, those whose hearts are evangelized—the shepherds, Mary, Joseph, Zachary, Elizabeth, Simeon, and Anna.

a. The Hidden Life

Matthew and Luke end their infancy narratives with an allusion to the hidden life. Luke speaks of it twice (2:39-40; 51-52). The episode of the loss of Jesus in the Temple at twelve years of age is, I think, what best reveals to us the significance and the secret of this saving existence. For long it seemed to be the most ordinary in the world, spent in the working life of an artisan; and it will last until the public life. Luke tells us that "Jesus, when he began his ministry, was about thirty years of age, being the son (as was supposed) of Joseph . . ." (3:23).

Luke is also the one who relates the incident of the journey to the Temple at the time when Jesus, now twelve, had reached the age of majority. He takes upon himself the offering formerly made through the intermediary of Mary and Joseph. "Did you not know that I must be in my Father's house?" Luke sees in the event which takes place at Jerusalem on the occasion of the Paschal Feast, with its three days of anguished search, a clear anticipation of the way of salvation which Christ chose in his obedience: obedience to the will of the Father, obedience unto death.

Salvation comes to us first and foremost through this lived-out consecration to the Father's work, to his will, whatever it may be. And there we find the essence of the message of these thirty years of hidden life: Christ saves the world through patient daily fidelity to the simple necessities of human existence totally offered and ordered to his Father. Christ saves us by living a life fully human, the ordinary human condition; but through the obedience of faith he makes of it a perfect homage of self to God—a homage whose crowning will consist in the public revelation of this mystery (in his public life and proclamation of the word) and also of its consummation in love which offers itself to the very end (in paschal mystery).

Karl Rahner has already said that the theology of the hidden life has not yet been fully worked out. If ever it is more completely studied, it will certainly be a theology of human existence, as sanctifying and saving because it is faithfully ordered and offered to the Father and his Son, the Life. It took Christ thirty years to announce this message and to teach us how to live our own human existence to its true potential. We rediscover the content of this message in the pages of the Gospels and in their many signs which help us trace the fidelity of this dedicated existence, a loving, laborious gift burning with the interior fire of the Holy Spirit.

In practice, for the contemplation of this stage, I invite the retreatant to consult the sources available to us, to reconstitute and accept this message of the existence of Christ, who lived and walked among us in the world and its daily life as we know it, doing good. I think it is possible to reconstitute this period of Christ's life on two levels.

On the level of daily life in Palestine, we know much more today about the concrete life Christ led, with regard to his time, to persons, to mentalities and ways of life.

On the wide sociological level which pertains to the political, cultural, and religious society of the period, it is also easier to know the characteristic features.

Finally, in regard to the life situations which were his and within which he matured for some thirty years in the real growth of which the Gospel speaks (a growth which was, no doubt, in openness and acceptance), we can arrive at some small understanding of the stages of development he went through as a genuine man. He was present to his time, in the midst of so much ignorance and surrounded by material and cultural poverty; also by social, political, and religious factions. Jesus' desire for his Father's work and its patient accomplishment in the long years of his growth perhaps throw some light on the meaning of the temptations in the desert which he later related to his disciples on the way up to Jerusalem, where the "hour" of fulfillment arrived under the disconcerting guise of "the Passion." This, too, is why the social fact of slavery, perhaps the best example of the hindrance to the freedom of the children of God that existed on nearly all levels, inspired Christ before he died, at the moment when he freely gave up his life. At the Last Supper it was the act of the "free servant" that he performed, wishing thereby to teach the Apostles that he had come to bring salvation by loving and that we love by serving and by giving ourselves for those we love.

I have often noticed that in everyday life a rather frequent turning of contemplative attention on Christ in his hidden life, that is, on him as a genuine human being leading an ordinary human life over a period of many years, produces a real taste for companionship with Christ, for ordinary life lived with him, lived in his presence. The life of each one of us is essentially and theologically a hidden life in union with Christ, and also a life within the creative plan of the Father which is in process of realization in the Spirit. This faithful, daily, humdrum, or varied life is itself the contact point for our participation in this fulfillment of the Kingdom of him who is "the Life." Contact with the Lord of daily life reveals to us the extreme value of our existence "in him." "For you have died, and your life is hid with Christ in God. When Christ who is our life appears, then you also will appear with him in glory" (Col. 3:3-4).

b. Suggested Readings

Some who are making a retreat in daily life have time to read. For this stage of the Exercises I suggest the following:

On the Incarnation, the Ignatian meditation (*SpEx*, [101-109]): the Prologue of John (see the commentary of D. Stanley, *A Modern Scriptural Approach*, ch. 10, pp. 94-109; *I Encountered God: The Spiritual Exercises with the Gospel of John*, ch. 2, pp. 41-54); H.U. von Balthasar, *Heart of the World*, ch. 2.

On the contemplation of the mysteries of the infancy: In my interpretation I make use especially of R. Laurentin, *Structure et théologie de Luc I-II* (Paris, 1957). [See also F. Prat, *Jesus Christ: His Life*, ch. 3, Ed.]

See also D. Stanley, *Modern Scriptural Approach*, ch. 2, "The Problem of the Infancy Narratives" (pp. 110-118), and ch. 12, "The Good News of Christmas" (pp. 119-128); M. Ledrus, *Thèmes pour les Exercices Spirituels*, Meditations nos. 18, 19, and 20, on "Jésus conçu dans l'humiliation" (Annunciation), "Jésus naît dans l'expérience de l'indigence" (Nativity), and "Jésus attendu" (Presentation in the Temple); J. Laplace, *An Experience of Life in the Spirit*, pp. 94-107.

On the hidden life: I recommend the first chapter of Gaston Salet, *Trouver le Christ* (Paris: Mappus, 1955); "Le Christ et la vie de tous les jours," pp. 9-31; Prat, *Life of Christ*, pp. 110-140.

To reconstruct the period when Christ was alive and to learn about the customs of the Jews, I recommend "On Customs of the Jews," in Daniel-Rops, *Daily Life in Palestine*.[2]

2   On the religious situation, see M. Simon, *Les sectes juives au temps de Jésus* (Paris: P.U.F., 1960).

On the political situation: Martin Hengel, *Victory over Violence: Jesus and the Revolutionists* (Fortress, 1973), and *Was Jesus a Revolutionist?* (Fortress, 1971).

Other articles: I recommend especially those which present the matter and give an introduction to the meaning of the mysteries; see the pertinent matter in the Biblical Bibliography of *Biblical Theology and the Spiritual Exercises*, pp. 353-355; e.g., on the Gospel passages on the Infancy, the Incarnation, the Annunciation, the Visitation and the Magnificat, Mary, Joseph, the Nativity, the Presentation in the Temple, Jesus at the age of twelve, the Hidden Life.

Chapter 7

INITIATION INTO PERSONAL DISCERNMENT:
THE IGNATIAN DAY

What I call the "Ignatian day" is that day which Ignatius devotes, during a retreat of thirty days, to those meditations which he composed himself with a very definite aim: to introduce his retreatant to the stage of "contemplation-election"—that is, to the experience of the election carried on during the days devoted to the contemplations on the events or "mysteries" in the public life of Christ. This stage, therefore, consists of two sets of exercises. The first set, on the Two Standards, the Three Classes of Men, and the Three Kinds of Humility ([135, 163, 164]), focuses on the exercitant's preparing his or her dispositions in view of a possible election. The second set, which runs concurrently with the deliberations on the election, consists of contemplations on selected events in the life of Christ.

In the structural plan of the thirty-day Exercises, the three meditations of the introduction to the election and discernment are all made on one day. But the thoughts and attitudes which they stimulate are also intended to be a constant background of attitudes and thoughts which interact with the contemplations on Christ's words and deeds for the rest of the Second Week.

When the Exercises are made in daily life, two or three weeks may well be given to the first set of meditations pertaining to the election— especially if the exercitant is to understand well the meaning of this Ignatian introduction and its two aims: (1) to help the exercitant to prepare his or her dispositions for a coming election and (2) to serve as a tenor of thought which will permeate the forthcoming contemplations on the public life of Christ.

A. The Place and Meaning of These Meditations in the Second Week

This set of Ignatian meditations (the Two Standards, Three Classes, and Three Kinds of Humility) is placed in between two self-contained groups of contemplations, those on the infancy narratives (the hidden life) and those on the proclamation of God's revelation (the public life). Here, on the objective level of revelation, we now pass from the assertion of the saving mission of Christ, in the visualized narratives in chapters 1 and 2 of Luke and Matthew, to Christ's official proclamation of the word, his announcement of the Message which comes as a challenge to the believer in his or her experience of journeying in the footsteps of Christ. Likewise, on the subjective level of our contemplation, we pass from "seeing" (that is, from striving to gain an "interior knowledge" of who Christ truly is) to "listening" to this living Word whom we desire to receive now more deeply, to the full extent of our personal capacity, of our spiritual consciousness —of the lucidity and generosity which come from our correspondence with grace. The proclamation of the word, in faith, is something always done in the present. For the retreatant it is a direct, present questioning of himself or herself which personalizes the present action of the Holy Spirit and which requires special dispositions of openness in the intellect and of receptivity in the will.

The exercitant is now in a twofold context: a present proclamation of the word or message accompanied by the action of the Spirit, and also a preparation of genuine dispositions of openness and receptivity. In this context Ignatius places his introduction to the important stage of parallel meditative reasonings about an election and prayerful contemplations of Christ the Savior in action. I think that Ignatius' meditations set up a twofold objective to this introduction: to verify the dispositions necessary for the rest of the experience and to give the retreatant an introduction to the subject matter or content about which he or she may be deliberating for an election.

1. Verification of One's Dispositions

Before entrance into this stage of contemplations and election, which consists in listening to the Word Incarnate in order to let oneself be moved by the Spirit, Ignatius asks the retreatant to submit to a kind of verification of his or her dispositions. There are many reasons for this. They are especially related to the realism of the retreat experience, which from the outset is linked to the person's spiritual history and the concrete data that goes into one's life experience.

The dispositions which the exercitant examines directly in the first of the three Ignatian meditations, the Two Standards, bear on the quality of openness to God's word, to its content and to its demands. Consequently, this search will attempt to discern what in the retreatant's own personality can most effectively block acceptance of the divine word and the concomitant action of the Holy Spirit.

As we see, Ignatius is, above all, proposing a day of discernment directly geared to the immediate dispositions needed for continuing the retreat experience, for submitting oneself to unconditional listening to the divine communications. He means "indifference," that habit whereby, instead of acting from whims, we refrain from decision until the reasons appear for choice of the better option. I have noticed that this day is a concrete initiation, more direct than the rest of the retreat experience, to the personalized discernment of spirits.

2. Introduction to the Content or Subject Matter of the Election

It is doubly right that this day of discernment take the form of an introduction to the content of the election, the options about which a good choice can be made. The Two Standards ([140-147]) casts a necessary light on the road toward electing to follow Christ more radically. It does this on the objective level by showing the demands and aims of Christ's actions or, in other words, by presenting a summary view of his program. Even if it is still presented in a very general manner, this is already precisely the path which the retreatant must follow if he or she wishes to hold fast to the truth of the Gospel revelation. In one way or other, in the immediate or remote future, he must make it the object of his choice, or learn to situate his other choices according to the enlightenment it gives.

On the subjective level, in many a case the subject matter of the election also takes on determining aspects. The experience of discerning is improved by the enlightenment just mentioned, which has a challenging quality. Hence the discernment pries into one's deep tendencies and possible areas of resistance to the word and to the Holy Spirit's graces. This too is a factor, and often the deciding one, in determining the object of one's personal election. The retreatant, by identifying or better discerning the personal trait which offers most resistance to grace (which is also the point of contact most sought by the evil spirit), often finds himself or herself directly oriented along the lines of the call which God addresses to him, today. By that call, conformed to the general aims of the gospel, God seeks to accomplish his deepest work of liberation. Here we come back to the area of the "foundational election," which bears on the readjustment necessary if the retreatant is to learn how to conform his or her personality as closely as possible to Christ and his way, and to confide all future progress to him.

The day of the Ignatian meditations, by means of the exercise of a methodical discernment carried out with the realism of a self-knowledge pushed to its limits, and in the objective light of the essential "intentions" of the Lord, forms a beginning, even on the level of the content concerned, for the very personal step of the election and readjustment. And the discernment of this readjustment will be discovered ever more clearly during the contemplations on the innumerable mysteries of the Gospel, under the moving impulses of the Holy Spirit.

Now let us see how each of these meditations proposed by St. Ignatius contributes to this important task of introduction to the process of discerning.

B. The Subject Matter of This Introductory Day

In the book of the Exercises, the concrete directives for each of the three Ignatian meditations should be viewed in regard to their place within the framework of the "thirty days." As these meditations theoretically take up only one day, Ignatius gives most importance and devotes the most time to the first of the three, the Two Standards. It constitutes, properly speaking, the exercise to verify the dispositions and introduce the content of the election. That is why he asks the retreatant to devote four of the five exercises of this day to it. The meditation on the Three Classes of Men closes this day of discernment on an exclusively prayerful note. It thus allows the person to take before God, in humble supplication, whatever precise point of resistance or repugnance the preceding exercise has brought into a clearer light. As for the Three Kinds of Humility, they are a "consideration" to be made during this day and also to be kept in mind during those which follow. They constitute a sort of accompaniment, of reflection in depth which brings about a continual repetition and deepening of the problem of dispositions—and particularly that of the availability required for the election, in other words, of that indifference which is here an unconditional acceptance of the ways of God.

1. The Two Standards

Before recalling the content of this well-known exercise, I should like to point out certain concrete details which orient its presentation and its being carried out in practice.

A first and very down-to-earth observation concerns the outdated language of Ignatius' era which often creates disproportionate obstacles.

This language must be purified; we must know how to disengage the important realities it contains. Underneath the rather old-fashioned symbolism of the "standards" or banners or flags, as well as that of the two "cities" of Babylon and Jerusalem, the prototypes of the "two kingdoms," we are faced with the problem of the fundamental options which have always pulled human beings in different directions—options for good or for evil, for life or for death, for Christ or for Satan, the living spirit of evil.

Another practical observation has its importance: The meditation on the Two Standards provides us, when its content is grasped in detail, with a background or framework of counsels and strategies which give us light for viewing other things. The meditation can be compared to a grating through which we view them. That is, we use this background and these strategies to test and verify our coming deliberations and the discernment which we desire. It is, if course, good to meditate on this background and thus deepen our grasp of its cogency, or realism, and the like. But it is far more important to search in prayer for the application of it to our personal life. With this application in view, Ignatius has us ask for an understanding of the wiles of Satan and the strategies of Christ, so that we may, by discerning them in our personal life, gain the courage to turn away from the oppressive force contained in the wiles in order to surrender ourselves ever more to the liberating strength of Christ's usual procedures. We should, therefore, take some time to understand the meaning of this background, for the criteria it suggests and for the procedures it points out for our instruction. But once this understanding has been gained to a reasonable extent, the real work to be done is one of prayerful seeking, in relation to our own concrete life, to our own psychological and spiritual functioning. We should investigate where these respective strategies of Christ and of Satan are being applied in our own life.

Now for a last remark, which will be more enlightening when we come to the content of this exercise. Our search must especially deal with the first item of the development we have analyzed (riches as opposed to poverty), whether we are considering the action of the Evil One or the strategies of Christ. For this first item is equivalently, on the one hand, attachment to self or self-will and, on the other, poverty (that is, interior freedom). The first item of contrast is so fundamental that of itself it ensures the existence and the vitality of the other items proposed by the analysis (insults versus empty honors, humility versus pride). Assuredly, it is not useless to seek for the concrete significance or import of these other items in our own personal life. Sometimes this might be even necessary, especially when light about the first item is hard to obtain. We then have recourse to them, somewhat as one studies effects and relates them to the cause. The other two items, better discerned in real life, can help toward understanding the first and grasping its true impact in our life. However, what really matters is to exercise this discernment taught by the Two Standards with regard to this first item or stage of the process of the development: riches to worldly honor to pride, or poverty to contempt to humility and the virtues it entails. This first item remains fundamental, a veritable stake in the game, whether on the negative side (the evil in ourselves) or the positive side (God's grace operating in us). As a proof, we have Ignatius' second meditation, that on the Three Classes of Men. It is exclusively concerned with the first item or stage, to bring it to greater maturity: deliverance from fundamental repugnances and a surer progress of interior freedom under the Holy Spirit's influence.

In regard to the subject matter of this exercise, which I have called the background in the light of which we view our coming deliberations, I shall limit myself here to a brief summary of it, by way of a reminder of matters well known which have been explained at length elsewhere.[1]

On the one side, the evil spirit acts fundamentally in us by trying to bind us, to attach us to something which ultimately is always our own self, no matter how many possible realities may be in between. Ignatius speaks of money, mammon, with St. Matthew; of riches with St. Luke; and of greed with St. Paul (1 Tim. 6:10). Under all these different expressions, as under the particular "goods" which captivate each person (material or spiritual goods, the body, health, beauty, work, accomplishments, ideas, opinions, friendship, esteem, perfection, or anything else), Ignatius is speaking of the instinct for possession. If this is not regulated, we seek through it to appropriate to ourselves something which we progressively identify as belonging and existing for ourselves. (See the First Week, where the explanation of evil comes to a head in this substitution of having for being.) This instinct of attachment to self by the subterfuge of "goods possessed" is fundamental in the process by which evil operates. It is on this sensitive point of attachment and hardening, which first of all binds us to ourselves, that we shall later confront others and demand, more or less consciously, to be recognized by others in regard precisely to this point of self-assertiveness—that which Ignatius calls "honor." By this subterfuge we come to prefer ourselves to others, to take up a position against others and against God; and this is the culmination of pride which kills.

For his part, Christ invites us throughout the Gospels to poverty of heart, to interior detachment and even to denial of self. Then failure to be recognized by others or even being misunderstood by them does not affect

---

1 *Biblical Theology and the Spiritual Exercises*, pp. 253-258.

our interior peace. Walking along this path, we learn to place ourselves more fully on the side of humility and renunciation, which, taken together, make us capable even of accepting humiliation if need be, and maintain us on the side of peace and of the love and praise reserved for the persecuted.

These are the two roads which open from within for man to follow. They have concrete implications, of which we can find very distinct evidences in our own past lives. Evidently, it is important when presenting the exercise of the Two Standards to explain these two paths more clearly, with their respective dynamisms and their concrete implications. Along the one we are caught up into a process of separation, isolation, and mortal self-sufficiency which constitutes sin as a profound attitude. This is the attitude which leads to acts of rupture and to sins of transgression. The other road contains in summary the whole of the gospel and leads to dispositions of patient progress in grace, progress which sustains the continual conversion and stripping of self demanded by love and life. "If a man wishes to find his life he will lose it, and he who loses his life will find it."

2. The Three Classes of Persons

As I have already stated, the meditation on the Three Classes or categories of Persons is the last of the five practical exercises on this Ignatian day. In one sense, it takes the place of the application of the senses which, on other such days, is usually added to the series of repetitions on some mystery. That is why we are inclined a priori to attribute to the Three Classes the more gratuitous, more passive and contemplative character which marked the last exercise of the other days of the Second Week, which came to their end with the application of the senses.

Ignatius' intention would seem to be in agreement with this supposition, since he makes of it a kind of prayerful return to the first item in the meditation on the Two Standards. We have only to look at the "preludes" of his meditation to be convinced of this. They deal with men who are involved in an attachment to some good which interferes with the peace of their union and gift of self to God; and the grace to be prayed for is to overcome the obstacle, the reason for the persons' repugnance and failure to experience peace. The antidote is a greater attachment to God and to his will. This meditation placed at the end of the day, therefore, seems to be a pressing invitation to prayer; to a lucid prayer guided by the view of this truth discerned in the course of the preceding exercises, and aimed at helping the retreatant to grow in a more total unconditional attachment to the will of God. Only this growing attachment to God will render one capable of overcoming the resistance or repugnance which one may still strongly feel.

Here too is where we find the purpose of this exercise. The consideration of the Three Classes or categories of persons at grips with this problem leads us rapidly to adopt the only possible solution, that of the third class of men. Persons in this category receive from God, beyond their own more or less adequate efforts, the grace of a greater interior desire which attaches them more closely to his will. Consequently, only persons in this category will, by means of grace, truly grow in the desired supernatural indifference. This indifference is then linked in practice to the concrete good which is the object of the present attachment, and brings the person to desire the will of God above everything else, whatever his will may be: either to sacrifice the good or to keep it and use it henceforth in an ordered fashion.[2]

3. The Three Degrees of Humility

I do not wish to delay here to justify the interpretation which I give to St. Ignatius' Three Kinds of Humility, also called modes, or species, or degrees of humility. I have done this elsewhere in detail.[3] Here I merely wish to point out with precision the role of this "consideration" during the exercises which will be proposed on the remaining days of the Second Week, and even beyond. I shall also give briefly the meaning of each of these three kinds. These three degrees specify the role which this "consideration" plays on each of the three levels through which the reality designated by the "three degrees" evolves. They are kinds of humility, yes, but also, in Ignatius' own language, degrees of love and of desire to serve God.

The overall role of this "consideration" (as distinct from a "meditation") is the following: to prolong, as a kind of constant background thought related to the activity of discernment, a reflection which proposes, in another way, the same criteria for verification of the retreatant's dispositions, and for opening these dispositions into a path which calls for ever more freedom and ever more availability for the following of Christ. Thus, not only does this additional verification, along with and by means of other forms of evaluation, make it possible to acquire a clearer understanding of the retreatant's interior situation, but it also opens up ways for the evolution of the availability which draws one to become more

2 See ibid., pp. 258-263.
3 See ibid., pp. 263-270.

and more conformed to Christ as our Savior. Thus this verification is a taking hold of the past and the present of one's own interior experience, and also an invitation and encouragement to a further generous advance, in any measure indicated by the Holy Spirit himself.

In this context let us remember that the first degree of love and of desire to serve God entails a humility and a capacity of self-renunciation that makes one ready to obey every law of God. To this degree corresponds obedience to God and all his laws, commandments, and precepts. The second degree brings one to desire not only to obey all the divine laws, but also to carry out all God's desires or indications which apply to one's own person, and to do this unconditionally. To this degree corresponds the indifference about which Ignatius often speaks. Finally, the third degree includes, not only this unconditional acceptance of anything for which God indicates his desire (whether sickness or health, a long life or a short one, to be a lawyer or a teacher), but in addition a loving option to be with Christ poor, suffering, mocked. That is the measure of the growth of the love which sustains us as we follow the paths of humility, self-renunciation, and dedication to the following of Christ.

A final remark about these degrees of humility. Care must be taken not to depreciate the second in order to reach the third more readily. True Ignatian indifference, necessary for hearing the word of God and for following Christ, is part of the second degree. One recognizes that it already contains everything and excludes nothing (such as health or sickness, or even death); but one does not state explicitly that this interior movement belongs to the third degree, comes from the Holy Spirit, and carries the person toward embracing the folly of the cross more closely. It happens that persons who are poorly directed ask for the third degree even though they lack this fundamental indifference in regard to many concrete factors in their life, and sometimes even in regard to the very object for which they are expressing their desire, namely, this third degree of humility. This third degree can be inspired by interior motions caused by the Holy Spirit (and this requires the exercise of a very delicate discernment of spirits); but it can also be necessary for dealing with concrete situations which should be accepted in this spirit—such as trials, failure, sickness, premature death, or what not else. For this reason, I wonder if we should not all aim interiorly, with realism, at this kind of humility, to the extent brought on when advancing age faces us with its concomitant inefficiency, inactivity, or seeming uselessness.

Finally, classic examples of the third degree, transmitted by a tradition of lives of saints more to be admired than imitated, have perhaps raised some expressions of this third degree into absolutes; and they have also relegated into obscurity other forms of high virtues which those saints quietly practice, even in lives where health and success flourish. For example, St. Ignatius expected all his sons, as religious, to opt for the effective poverty "with Christ poor" and, in consequence, to strive "to feel the effects of this poverty" in their personal life, which continues to be ordered to apostolic works. On condition that they respect all the possibilities offered by the third degree in its expansive scope (and this remains an "option for the suffering Christ"), I am more and more inclined to believe, with Ignatius, that persons who have dedicated themselves to the spread of the Kingdom should be disposed to arrive at the third kind of humility. Perhaps this confers an unsuspected depth to the Ignatian conception of the religious life, and a radical character to the evangelical commitment which it signifies in the following of Christ.

C. Some Practical Observations

"To finish this chapter where I began it," here are some conclusions or practical observations on the whole of this "Ignatian day" devoted to spiritual discernment and to the introduction to the election.

1. Attachment to Self—the Devil's First Deceit

At first, once the problem has been well stated, it is wise to point out Satan's first objective in his deceits. Usually, he does not aim at a person's most frequent occasions of sinning, or at his most grievous failings, or at his or her chief weak point. Rather, he chooses one of the person's real or imaginary forms of "riches" or attachment to self which puts him in danger of separating himself most effectively from others and from God. It happens that those who have made the Exercises often and who are accustomed to this series of temptations mentioned in the Two Standards, frequently linger on something which is weakness, temptation, or a heavy cross to bear in life, rather than on that subtle snare of "wealth" as the attachment deadly to themselves. It is good to counter this deceit and to invite these persons to renew their discernment with regard to the sources of evil in their lives.

2. The Dispositions Chiefly for This Period in the Retreat Experience

A second remark should be made. As we have already seen, the whole of this day (which is extended over several weeks in the case of the Exercises made in daily life) aims at evaluating one's indifference. ("Indifference" is here taken in Ignatius' sense of a decision withheld until the finding of the reasons that reveal which option is truly better; this indifference is also called "interior freedom.") This indifference is equivalent to an unconditional openness to the requirements of God's revealed word, to the action of the Spirit, to the divine good pleasure as perceived by the procedures of the election. We must, however, guard against a misunderstanding which often immobilizes a retreatant. While testing the inevitable limitations of his or her own indifference, he hesitates in fact to declare himself sufficiently available (especially if he is something of a perfectionist) to continue this retreat experience. Did not St. Ignatius point out in his autograph Directory that "the retreatant who has not attained the indifference of the second degree of humility should not begin the elections"? Therefore, the error to be avoided is that of considering the present evaluation of one's dispositions to refer, even in a global way, to one's whole future life. The matter under consideration at this point, if one is to be permitted to continue the Exercises, is not that of installing oneself definitively in a state of permanent and unconditional availability. Who would ever attain this? The matter under consideration, therefore, is the present moment of experience, that in which one would sincerely commit oneself to listen attentively to God's word in the immediate discernment carried out here and now during this Ignatian day. We should look to the future only to realize more clearly the degree of resistances flowing from one's own personality. In this same measure, the prayer which begs deliverance is that about the present moment, so that one may hear God's word or message correctly, and will extend it into the future on any occasion when the same freedom will be needed, along with God's prevenient and salutary grace. It is a fact that all freedom, dearly bought, must be won over and over again, in this domain as in every other. Let us remember, then, that it is the present moment of the retreat experience that is first of all brought into question here and submitted to any necessary purification.

3. The Language Used

Along the same line as the preceding warnings, we ought to pay attention to the language we use when we speak of indifference. Above all, we should avoid vividly proposing as immediately threatening us those cases which Ignatius quotes merely as examples to help us to understand what indifference means: health or sickness, a long or a short life, failure or success, honor or dishonor, humiliations or even martyrdom. The subject of reflection and of evaluation should be our overall attitude of indifference, or unconditional offering, and not these possible objects of theoretical indifference. Often such considerations are not at all realistic.

In order to avoid this stumbling block, which would deprive indifference of its present impact and its realistic content, it is better to look for examples in the life of the person concerned; he or she will better concretize the meaning of this attitude to be acquired or developed. There will be less risk of frightening the retreatant with representations that are possibly false. Far more importantly, we shall orient the growth of this interior attitude in a realistic way by making it bear on a concrete personal matter rather than some imagined future.

4. The Possibility of Prolonging These Meditations

Finally, as we have seen, Ignatius states that the work of the election should not be undertaken if this fundamental attitude of indifference is not sufficiently acquired at the point presently reached in the retreat. If God's word is listened to only with mental reservations and with ifs and buts, it completely deafens us to his true questionings and makes us impermeable to the Holy Spirit's action. Hence Ignatius suggests that the retreatant be kept on these or similar meditations for as long a time as is necessary— similar, no doubt, to the Two Standards and the Three Classes of Men. But it might also be advantageous to go back to the mysteries of the hidden life (the infancy narratives), because the aim of these contemplations was a more radical attachment to Christ and to his ways. It is by these methods that genuine availability for an unconditional acceptance of God's word or message spiritually matures.

5. Some Suggestions on Prayer

During this period of very personal discernment, prolonged more or less in accordance with cases, the matter of the retreatant's discernment serves also as the subject matter of his or her prayer. It is that in the third prelude of the Two Standards (to know the deceits of the devil and the strategy of Christ) and of the Three Classes of Men (grace to choose what is more to the glory of God and to my salvation and spiritual growth).

Some texts of Scripture could profitably be used, especially when the period of discernment must be prolonged a bit. These are fitting occasions of reflection or of direct inspiration from prayer which has learned to draw its nourishment from Scripture. With this in view, I suggest texts on the theme of discernment as St. Paul presents it to the Ephesians (5:8-14). Since this discernment is in itself an effort, with the grace of God, to situate ourselves in the light which takes us out of our own darkness, I also propose the texts of St. John which exhort us to make a radical option for the Light in Christ; for example, John 8:12 and parallel texts, such as John 3:19-21 and 1 John 1:5-7; 2:8-11, and others similar.

Finally, as accompanying reading and inspirational background for discernment carried out in the spirit of the Gospel, Matthew 13:3-30 can be prayerfully considered with much fruit. Here Christ gives us the parable of the sower and that of the cockle and wheat. In the same sense, one could pray the first Psalm on "the two ways."[4]

Moreover, it must not be forgotten that the contemplations on the public life will often bring us back, if necessary, to the radical demands of the following of Christ expressed in his discourses and parables:

> "He who would come after me, let him deny himself. If your eye causes you to sin, pluck it out. No one who puts his hand to the plow and looks back is fit for the kingdom of God. He who loves father or mother more than me is not worthy of me. Go, sell what you have and give to the poor, . . . and come, follow me."

4   J. Laplace also presents Scriptural texts for prayer (such as Wis. 8:17-19, 18, Beatitudes, etc.) and accompanies them with reflections on discernment. See Laplace, *Life in the Spirit*, pp. 98-144.

Chapter 8

THE PUBLIC LIFE:
CONTEMPLATIONS ON GOSPEL EVENTS
AND SIMULTANEOUS DELIBERATIONS FOR AN ELECTION

For two reasons stage 5b (see Figure 2 above, in chapter 2), which we are entering now, can easily become one of the longest of the entire retreat experience. It ought to help the retreatant to bring the following of Christ, which is a "growing in Christ," to a peak in his or her own personal life. It will achieve this by drawing its matter or objective nourishment for this task from contemplation of the many mysteries in the public life of Christ; in other words, from that period which in each Gospel extends from the preaching of the Baptist to the Last Supper exclusively (see Matt. 3-25; Mark 1-13; Luke 3-21; John 1-12). This is the second block of exercises for the revealing of Christ, to fulfill a specific role (that is, a particular fundamental aim and function) in the believer's retreat experience. We shall have recourse to this dynamic thrust of the revealing process to throw light on the same impulse of the faith experience, and to give it the nourishment it needs for its follow-up in the Spirit.

A. The Meaning of This Stage

To keep the dialectical reasoning we have been using, let us first of all examine the universal aspect which will throw a better light on the retreatant's concrete subjective progress at this point in the retreat. Then let us examine this dynamic progression of God's revealing process (which in the present case is our "universal" aspect), in order to decide the import and the principal requirements of the present stage, namely, that of contemplations on events in Christ's life and of parallel deliberations about an election or choice which the exercitant may have to make.

1. The Sociological and Spiritual Significance of the Public Life

From the sociological point of view, the public life of Christ constitutes a historical fact circumscribed within limits of time and space, established, measurable, and having a precise human content. This concerns the last period of Jesus' life, when, at about the age of thirty and impelled by the Holy Spirit, he manifested himself in public. In other words, it was when he began to proclaim God's word. As we know, he disturbed many people, entire classes both political and religious; and this led him to a premature death, leaving behind him a small group of rather puzzled disciples.

From the spiritual point of view, it is the faith dimension of this same history that we accept. There is a perfect analogy between the sociological and the spiritual meanings of Christ's public life on the one hand and, on the other, the problem of the historical Christ and the Christ of faith. In fact, in the faith we believe that Christ's proclamation of God's word to which we refer here did not cease with his death. To this historical, concrete proclamation corresponds the ever-living proclamation by the Church of Christ, the Word of God ceaselessly revealing his Father and his Kingdom, the way of our salvation and its demands. While heaven and earth will pass away, the word will remain—a word proclaimed continuously. In the faith, too, each person can become present to this ever-present word which is always being proclaimed anew at the present moment. Memory, philological knowledge, and exegesis intervene only to recover from the past the medium of communication (that is, the history, language, culture, literary style, personality of the writer, and the like) which transmits to us now Christ the living Word always present to us.

The public life, seen from the viewpoint of our faith, is the object of contemplation during the Second Week. The other view, the historical one, furnishes the medium necessary for communication in this realm of incarnation. Consequently, we ought to contemplate from this viewpoint of faith, more than by means of our memory, imagination, and perceptive powers. These faculties, useful in themselves, are an aid to find, carry, or accept that medium of communication and the message it contains, transmitted in human language. To contemplate by means of an enlightened, conscious, and accepting faith is to welcome this reality pronounced today through the intermediary of means coming from the past. Contemplation is an activity to be fully carried out by active faith, whatever may be its effect on the imagination and feelings. It is always a free act of presence to this word spoken or carried out in action, ever present and addressed to me at the moment when, aided by faith, I turn to listen to it. From this free acceptance, which is always possible, is born a life related to God; and this consists in God himself making his dwelling within us.

2. The Function of the Mysteries of the Public Life in Divine Revelation and in the Christian Experience

Jesus told us that he came so that all might have life and have it in abundance. The glory of God, according to Maxim the Confessor, is "the life of man." We have had the opportunity, when considering the Principle and Foundation, of becoming familiar with this mystery of hope and life. We were then drawn onwards to live more fully in accordance with this unifying vision arising from our Christian faith. The deepening of this vision is both an objective and a result of our spiritual experience. We have also seen that the mysteries or events in Christ's public life directly reveal to us more and more clearly just who he is and the doctrine he taught. Thus they foster our growing assimilation of the life he offers. His life on earth, his words and deeds, are given to us so that we may come to know him as God, be born to his life, and progress towards that fullness of existence where, with the whole of creation, he will form the eternal Kingdom of God—a kingdom of peace, justice, love, and life. "This is eternal life, that they know thee the only true God, and Jesus Christ whom thou hast sent" (John 17:3).

The mysteries of the public life of Christ belong directly to this dynamic progression in the gradual revealing of Christ to us. They become a very pressing call to follow Christ, the way and the life of the Kingdom. When he began to speak, Christ revealed to us many aspects of the Kingdom hitherto comparatively unknown, such as God's plan of human salvation through Christ, St. Paul's "mystery of Christ." He told us what the Kingdom is, who is invited to it, how it can be entered or taken by storm, and how to live here below while awaiting its fullness in him at the end of time. The Gospels bring us this Word Incarnate and his spoken words. They continue to recount and to construct the Kingdom for us, and to invite us by name while indicating the way we should follow. That is why the mysteries of the public life of Christ, in faith, through a living encounter rather than through any kind of demonstration, teach us life and initiate us into the way to take to live in Christ.

The first fruit to be expected from the contemplation of the public life —a contemplation which is a listening to, and an acceptance of, the Living Word—will, then, be to teach us to allow ourselves to be challenged personally (while taking account of our own past on which we shall build), in order to accept the Kingdom and permit it to grow in us. This growth, gratuitous like the gift and life of God, will take place only on condition that we pay the price of our freedom and commitment "in spirit and in truth." For this Kingdom is that precious pearl for which everything is worth sacrificing, that divine seed which is small but powerful. Like the inexorable yeast, it has the power to grow in spite of the persistent conflict between the seeds of cockle and the good seeds of wheat. It is the eternal life of Christ transmitted, through faith and communion, to persons of goodwill. It is God's dwelling within ourselves.

Another important component of the Kingdom and of the following of Christ through the mysteries of his public life is the concomitant action of the Holy Spirit upon us through his graces, those lights in our intellects and impulses in our wills. Because it is living, the spoken word is always accompanied by the Spirit.[1] If the spoken words communicate an objective content or message which we should receive with great respect—as one welcomes the Divine Majesty itself, St. Ignatius said—the Spirit comes with his graces to help us apply those words to ourselves. He reaches us through those words, works in us according to his desires, transforms us, and finally changes us completely for the glory of God and our own greater good.

So it is to a truly living personal encounter that the believer offers himself when he or she receives the revealed word in full lucidity, whether it comes to him through sacred reading, prayer and contemplation, the celebration of the liturgy, or otherwise. This is the activity that Ignatius proposes directly to his retreatant during the Second Week and at this point of the experience of the Exercises.

3. The Contemplations and the Simultaneous Deliberations for an Election

To conclude the foregoing, we can give its full significance to the expression "contemplation-election," which sums up the activity proper to this stage, on the objective and on the subjective levels. On the subjective level this activity consists in accepting the word or message (through contemplation) and in submitting to the action of the Spirit (particularly in regard to an election[2] which may be in view).

In fact, by respecting God's intention in his revelation and the place which he allotted to the mysteries of the public life in the corpus of his revelation, the retreatant of the Second Week, like a believer challenged by this revealed word, will exercise his activity of contemplation. Here this consists in listening to and accepting a present, living word addressed to him as something to be read from the viewpoint of his or her faith.

Likewise, by submitting to the graces of the Holy Spirit, who always

---

1   *Biblical Theology and the Spiritual Exercises*, pp. 239-243.

2   On interior renewal or the reformation of life as a purpose of the *Exercises* and a form of election, see *Biblical Theology and the Spiritual Exercises*, pp. 81-93, esp. pp. 85-87.

accompanies this living word (proclaimed and accepted), this same retreatant will carry on the deliberations towards the choices to which he or she will be drawn by his spiritual experience, now brought more into his awareness by the preceding exercises and by his wish to correspond with the desires of God for him. This is the meaning of the election.

Hence as the days of contemplations progress, the election will become proportionately more concrete, more mature, and more likely to bear the expected fruits of conversion, adjustment in faith, and commitment for the Kingdom, in accordance with the way God is leading this person here and now to build upon his or her own spiritual history.

B. The Contemplations on the Gospel Mysteries: The Hearing of the Word and Acceptance of It

To make my treatment clearer, I shall comment separately first on the series of contemplations on the Gospel mysteries, and subsequently on Ignatius' series of directives and criteria for an election. For ordinarily the deliberations on an election evolve concurrently with the contemplations and in strict dependence upon them. In the same way, acceptance of the revealed message and openness to the Holy Spirit naturally go hand in hand through the remainder of the Second Week.

We already know several things about the contemplation of the mysteries of the Second Week, for example, its aim, which the dynamism of the revealed message enlightens so that it stimulates a deeper experience of faith. Likewise, beyond the problems about methods of contemplation (a topic which is usually better understood at this point of the experience), there is question of the basic procedure which makes of the retreatant's contemplation an activity of his presence in faith to the events, and integrates the work of his other faculties, without being limited to their level of expression. To these matters, which I feel are most important for the full benefit of the experience, I shall add some proposals on the distribution of the subject matter in the Second Week. I shall do this by referring to three possible principles of distribution of the Gospel mysteries which are offered for the contemplation of the retreatant.

1. The First Principle on the Objective Level for the Selection of the Gospel Mysteries: The Internal Logic in Christ's Proclamation of His Kingdom

The first principle embraces the whole of the revelation made in the Gospels, and seeks to trace the dynamism of this revelation in direct relationship with its content. The Kingdom, which is salvation and our spiritual life, the primary objective of this revelation, is announced progressively and explained to our mind and heart through the Messiah who reveals it and carries it into effect among us. By way of suggestion, I should say that a distribution of the subject matter according to this principle could be made as follows:

    a. *Mysteries pertaining to Christ's Own Messianic Commitment*: Christ himself is called, under the motion from the Holy Spirit, to break the privacy of his hidden life, to begin to speak out, to accomplish the hour of salvation. Faithful to the Spirit who inspires him, he accepts and, lined up with sinners, he sets in motion the Messianic struggle which involves all of us. (We see this in the preaching of the Baptist, the baptism of Jesus, and his temptation in the desert.)[3]

    b. *Christ's Call for Our Sharing in His Mission*: Jesus cannot accomplish the work of salvation alone; he involves in his task those whom he has come to save. He needs disciples and, with them, he begins the formation of that living body which will become his Kingdom and Church—his Mystical Body transmitting his salvation to others through the centuries. (We see this in the various calls of the apostles in the Gospel, especially in John 1:19-34, as well as in his different approaches to persons, the answers given, and the like.)[4]

    c. *The Signs of the Messianic Era and the Progressive Revelation of the Kingdom*: This revelation can start, for example, with the wedding feast at Cana, universal in character, when in the fullness of time the Messianic era is inaugurated in the manner of the banquet of the poor announced through Isaiah (ch. 55) and continues down to one's free, personal commitment to it, as radical as one's first birth (see the Nicodemus episode in John 2 and 3). This kingdom is announced through multitudinous signs (cures and raisings from the dead, pardons and exorcisms)—signs of power, of kindness, of confirmation in faith.[5]

    d. *The Gospel Doctrine and the Requirements for Being a "Follower of Christ" (of Living in Christ)*: This doctrine, already stated in all the preceding, is further explained through the parables (those of the Kingdom) and the discourses (the many demands of this mystery of

3 On the subject of the baptism and the temptations of Jesus, see Stanley, *Modern Scriptural Approach*, chs. 13 and 14, pp. 129-146.

4 See Alban Goodier, *The Public Life of Our Lord Jesus Christ* (London, 1931), vol. 1, ch. 4, no. 6, "The First Disciples," pp. 33-45.

5 See D. Mollat, *Initiation à la Lecture Spirituelle de saint Jean* (1964).

life).[6] It entails the requirements for "living in Christ," that is, in his Mystical Body, the Church.

2. The Second Principle on the Objective Level for the Selection of the Gospel Mysteries: The Four Approaches of the Evangelists in Composing Their Respective Gospels

We know that each evangelist gives witness, not only of his own personality which colors his way of transmitting the message, but also of his own aim, theological reflections, and preoccupations, often adjusted to the precise audience whom he was addressing. Thus we have Matthew and the Jews, Mark and the catechesis of Peter, Luke and his universalism, John and the deep theological insights of his "spiritual Gospel." No doubt the particular line followed by any one of the four Gospels can impart a certain unity and fecundity to the contemplation of the mysteries during the Second Week.[7]

3. Another Principle for Selection, on the Subjective Level: The Internal Dynamism of the Retreatant's Spiritual Experience

As the spiritual experience develops, progresses, and becomes more and more personal, the retreatant himself or herself will experience desires to contemplate this or that Gospel topic, especially when these contemplations are being carried on during a retreat made in everyday life. This internal dynamism, however, should not bypass the great basic meditations on the Messianic commitment of Christ and the inauguration of the era of salvation. But once the proclamation of the Kingdom has been covered and a prolonged pondering of Christ through the events of his life has begun, it happens that the current experience and the spiritual preference of the retreatant bring personal needs or desires to mind. The logic of the sacred writings should not be a block to satisfying such needs. Attention should be paid to this life experience and to its signs in order to follow the movement of the Spirit which is often entailed therein.

---

6 See Stanley, *Modern Scriptural Approach*, ch. 16 (Sermon on the Mount), pp. 158-165. Also for other studies on the public life, Biblical Bibliography in *Biblical Theology and the Spiritual Exercises*, pp. 355-361.

7 See *Biblical Theology and the Spiritual Exercises*, pp. 219-233, with reference to the articles of F. J. McCool and J. A. Fitzmyer on this subject. F. J. McCool, "The Preacher and the Historical Witness of the Gospels," *Theological Studies*, 21 (1960), 517-543, reprinted in *The Modern Approach to the Gospel and the Spiritual Exercises* (New York: Fordham University Press, 1961), pp. 167-199; J. A. Fitzmyer, "The Spiritual Exercises of St. Ignatius and Recent Gospel Study," *Woodstock Letters*, 91 (1962), 246-274.

4. Practical Conclusions

I shall conclude this reflection on the choice and distribution of the mysteries to be contemplated by insisting on this flexibility which has been discussed just above. Without going counter to the laws of exegetical and theological interpretation, it may happen that the dynamism of a living encounter escapes these laws or goes beyond them. That is why we should remember that all our suggestions about the objective level have as their purpose to promote the retreatant's genuine encounter, a genuine faith experience. This experience takes place very often during the Exercises made in everyday life, in which the activity of the contemplations and the deliberations about a possible election can be spread out over a period of two to four or five months and can pass through fluctuations which are rarely thought of during a shorter and intensive retreat.

Thus I have noticed that, in this context, it was sometimes a good thing to leave aside a chosen line (for example, that of a particular Gospel which was found stimulating for a certain time) in order to give variety—not only by having recourse to another sacred author (which is sometimes helpful), but by tackling in a different way the same matter, which remains a source for an encounter with God, for example, by changing to a continuous reading of a whole Gospel in a calm, contemplative spirit.[8]

Finally, it is understood that within the same context of prolonged exercises the liturgy can play an exceptional part as a source of renewal and encounter. This is especially true when fraternal sharing in Christ takes place. It directly intensifies various aspects of the Christian experience.

C. The Work of the Election: Submission to the Action of the Holy Spirit

Here I shall deal with three concrete problems concerning the election in the Second Week; namely, the amount of time to be given to the election, the different levels of election, and the optimum conditions for its realization.

---

8 Some suggestions of general reading on the public life: I recommend chapter 3 of Balthasar, *Heart of the World*, "The Broken Sun," pp. 58-72; meditation no. 26 of *Ledrus*, and lesson no. 20 of *Corso*.

1. The Amount of Time to Be Given to the Election

In practice, the entire second half of the Second Week (or "fifth stage" of the road of the whole retreat) is given to the election. That is, after the contemplation of the mysteries of the infancy, and immediately after the "Ignatian meditations" on the Standards and Classes, which serve as an introduction to this stage of contemplations and election, there begins the prolonged contemplation of the mysteries of the public life which influence the development of the election. Thus the retreatant, in conformity with the dynamism of the topics revealing the proclamation of Christ's mission and Kingdom, is moved by the Spirit who always accompanies the word proclaimed. For the entire time that this contemplation lasts, he will literally be in a period of election or deliberations pertaining to choice.

However, it is important, within this period of contemplation-election, to determine a specified time to gather the more definite fruits of the election. Practically, this takes place when the progression of the Exercises makes the time seem ripe. Then the retreatant proceeds according to the methods and criteria described by St. Ignatius ([135, 169-189]). These include examples of objects of choice, an analysis of basic attractions, then the alternations between consolation and desolation, and a time of tranquility for a detailed examination which gathers together the accumulated facts. In other words, it is the time to take stock in a more methodical way, to see the point one has reached. This fairly short time—a period of a few hours, a day or longer if necessary—enables one to conclude the election temporarily; that is, to gather its fruit as it is, so that, submitting it to divine approbation (see [183]), one may move towards a new stage in the experience of the Exercises.

2. Levels of the Election

In the previous chapter I spoke of the introduction to the election by way of discernment of what entices us to take a vigorous step forward; and at that point I mentioned the foundational election. Practical experience has taught me to make the distinction which I now propose here. It is important, it seems to me, to distinguish clearly between two different levels of election in order to reach our aim in a more orderly fashion. These two levels constitute the foundational election and some secondary ones. The "foundational election" is often situated on the level of our deep personal attitudes, whereas the "secondary elections" lie rather on the level of means—notwithstanding the problem of elections which may bear on precise decisions to be made.

The foundational election is, then, of primary importance. If well carried out, it roots and orients all the secondary elections (of "decision" or of "means"). This is quite understandable since it corresponds to a fundamental adjustment of our whole personal selves in order to make ourselves as similar to Christ as possible and thus make sure of our future life in Christ and in his Mystical Body. However, this continual readjustment of self should not be envisaged in too general or global a fashion, confined to merely an overall survey of our own personality. Quite the contrary! The discernment which the Ignatian day envisaged aimed precisely at the vital center of the readjustment called for; and it further endeavored to identify concretely what might constitute an obstacle in the retrcatant's own case to a more total configuration to Christ. Positively, this discernment already gave an orientation towards an energetic step forward in the following of Christ, and that in regard to a matter no less precise.

Hence, it is important to give the fundamental election all the time required. For it is what will guide the person towards a full and realistic commitment to wholehearted following of Christ, no matter what other decisions this will entail. Through its light the other choices will be firmer and more enlightened. These other choices which the experience may make necessary by way of secondary elections, are usually of two kinds: (1) necessary and immanent decisions with which the retreatant is faced, such as examination or choice of a state of life, volunteering for a foreign mission, or anything similar; (2) the means to be taken in order to assure fidelity to the fundamental election, such as prayer, regular times of recollection, the use of spiritual direction, or the like. With regard to this latter point, the election dealing with means to be employed, it is good to be very functional and learn to choose fewer and better means rather than to take everything and then accomplish nothing in the end.

3. Conditions for Realizing the Election

Here we are dealing with a matter that is better known. Let us just recall the care St. Ignatius took to protect the time of a retreatant's election in order to make it a time of interior and exterior silence, a special time of meeting with the Lord and of attention to the Holy Spirit's delicate action in one's soul.

Here some remarks are in order on the topic of ensuring the best conditions for making a good election. To enable the retreatant to remain as much as possible in a state of "making a good choice" during the entire period devoted to these deliberations, it may no doubt be fitting to make some observations about the discernment of spirits of which Ignatius speaks in the Exercises ([313-336]). But in this regard, as also in regard to applying Ignatius' methods to the moment of concluding an election, I can only refer to his rules ([170-189], and specifically [183, 188, 189]), which constitute a valuable set of directives to guide the experience in progress. Still further, I have always thought that it was much easier to apply these rules of discernment to the concrete cases as they come up, rather than to speak of them in a general way. I might also say that in practice I never choose in advance the time that I shall spend in initiating a retreatant into the discernment of spirits. Rather, I feel my way toward this by noticing what turns up in the retreatant's day-to-day life. That is where the motions induced by the different spirits appear, and above all where one can learn to be sensitive to the action of the Holy Spirit.

The contemplation of the Gospel mysteries constitutes a natural parallel activity to these deliberations about an election. If necessary, certain reading might sometimes be suggested as a help to a more enlightened commitment.[9]

D. Transition from the End of the Election to the Third Week

Let us first of all say that, when the fruit of the election has been gathered and given a clear shape (for example, in a written text which defines and fixes it, at least in a tentative form, in the retreatant's mind and memory), it is good to proceed to a search for confirmation (likewise temporary) of the kind that Ignatius suggests in the *Exercises* ([183]). He asks his retreatant to go immediately to present himself before God in prayer, and to offer Him his or her choice so that the Divine Majesty may deign to accept and confirm it.

But this necessity of a deeper confirmation gives rise to the problem of the transition to be made between the termination of the election and the entry into the Third Week of the making of the Exercises.

It would, in fact, be premature to think that once the election is decided the retreatant is necessarily ready to go on to the next stage, that of Christ's Passion. The period which is coming to its end was something more than the problem of an election; it was a period of "contemplation-election." The retreatant's development should be assured on both these levels.

Up to this point the contemplation has been carried on, pretty directly,

---

9   With this in view I sometimes have recourse to two chapters of Balthasar, *Heart of the World*, ch. 7, "The Intruder," pp. 117-132, and ch. 8, "Jailhouse and Cocoon," pp. 133-144. As a brief and clear commentary on the procedure and methods of election, I recommend Laplace, *Life in the Spirit*, pp. 108-141.

along the dynamism of the gradual revealing of Christ and his mission. This drama advances step by step into the Passion; and the retreatant will do well to continue to keep herself or himself under the influence of its movement. This is the transition to be effected between the contemplations for hearing and accepting the message of Christ (the source of the election) and this "going up to Jerusalem" to which the following of Christ leads us.

Thus by following the interior dynamic in God's gradual revelation of his incarnate Son to the Jews of that day and then to all the gentiles (this gradual ascent towards what will be the object of contemplation during the Third Week), the retreatant will discover a firmer, surer confirmation of his or her own election. For he will normally make this transition in continuity with the internal dynamism of his own personality and past experience. Then, in line with his or her own election, which has now become the personal and concrete path of his commitment to following Christ, she or he will live and go up to Jerusalem in company with Christ. This will be the occasion of a new confirmation, but on condition of a lived experience of "going up to Jerusalem" until the retreatant's sharing in the paschal mystery with Christ awakens a response still more decisive.

As the concrete matter for this final step of the Second Week, one might use the following mysteries: the three announcements of the Passion (Mark 8:9-10), with the mystery of the Transfiguration[10] (which is inserted here as an appeal to faith within this mystery of the going up to death); the raising of Lazarus from the dead (John 11:1-57), which is a mystery of light and life through the very experience of death; the facing of death by Jesus, who announces and interprets what is coming (Mark 12:1-12, the murderous vinedressers); finally, the entry into Jerusalem (Matt. 21:1-17).

10   See Stanley, *Modern Scriptural Approach*, ch. 20, pp. 194-205.

THE THIRD AND FOURTH WEEKS:
AN EXPERIENCE OF SHARING
IN THE PASCHAL MYSTERY

With the paschal mystery (The Third and Fourth Weeks of the Exercises) begins the third and last stage of the long process of assimilation of which we spoke above, and the sixth stage of the whole road of the Exercises (see Figure 2 above, in chapter 2). I shall treat it as one single chapter, perhaps long, in order to show the unity of this final step, one of "communion" or intimate sharing.

What most characterizes this sixth and last stage of assimilation will be better understood if we review the progression of the preceding stages. In the first stage we started by clarifying the fundamental vision which springs from our Christian faith. In the second stage this bird's-eye view took in an interpretation of the problem of evil; and in the third stage it focused on Christ as King and Savior, who makes possible the achievement of the whole plan of God in the supernatural order. We then took up stage four, one of assimilation which followed the interior dynamic of the process by which God gradually revealed his Son to the Jews and then to the gentiles. People came to see the Savior through whom God's salvific plan was realized.

This first stage of our road in the Second Week was one of "seeing," that is, of contemplating the infancy narratives, in order to grow in interior knowledge of Christ and in loving attachment to his person. Then there was the stage of "listening" to the word which he officially proclaimed, to which the Gospel revelations invited us in view of surrendering ourselves to the Spirit to following Christ—in a manner which was growing ever more personal and also consonant with the objective demands of his Kingdom.

As we now come to the sixth stage, the summit of this revealing journey, divine revelation offers us for our contemplation during the Third and Fourth Weeks the saving act of Jesus, his paschal mystery. Contemplation, besides being knowledge ("seeing") and hearing ("election") should now be carried into action, that is, into communion with Christ, intimate fellowship with him. The communion in view is a close association with him in his paschal mystery. This is the point we must understand if we wish to pursue the true aim of this last stage of the retreat experience in these last two Weeks. We must now not only make ourselves present to see and listen to Christ (this must still be continued), but we should also dispose ourselves to participate in this saving act of Christ in a manner of communion still to be specified. In other words, now we must not only contemplate, but we must experience the Passion—and this on a deep level of existential communion which rises far above that of sympathy and sentiment. Therefore I shall take time here to explain, as I do in practice with my retreatants, the meaning of this aim: "to experience the Passion" in the Third Week. The same explanation holds good for the Resurrection mysteries in the Fourth Week. Then it is *in this perspective* that I shall briefly propose the subject matter of the exercises to be made in each of these Weeks, and I shall draw some conclusions on the subject of the concrete spiritual fruits which pertain to this closing stage of the Exercises.

A. The Experiential Character of This Stage

By conforming ourselves to the dynamism of revelation itself, we shall discover the form of contemplation suitable for this stage, which should include something more than the knowledge and acceptance of the mysteries revealed in the Third and Fourth Weeks.

1. The Dynamic Purpose of the Paschal Mystery in Divine Revelation

As we have seen, in God's evolving process of revelation, the infancy narratives aimed at making us know, beyond appearances, or rather through the medium of them, just what Christ as Savior really was: the divine Word Incarnate. This was the profound root from which his saving message and act sprang. The words he spoke, in the gradual unfolding of his public life and the proclamation of the Kingdom, then became a challenge in faith and a call to the believer to a present, effective conversion. But it is in the summit act by which he saved us that the Savior's task and our following of him find their chief fulfillment. Further, the permanence of this act is assured for ourselves by the eternal New Covenant established between God and humanity in Christ and by the communion made possible by our energized faith and our participation in the rite which makes present among us both Christ's expiatory sacrifice on the cross and the everlasting Eucharist by which he extends it to all humanity and makes it present among us. He does this in his capacity as the head of all humanity and of the whole of creation (1 Cor. 15:22-28). What then will be the form of contemplation suitable to this stage of assimilating the content of God's revelation? I have stated it in one word —it will be "communion," but communion accomplished through our energetic exercise of faith as much as by our gazing with love on our Savior as he goes through the events of his paschal mystery. For it is our spirit of faith, directly cultivated through this stage of the spiritual experience of the Exercises, which will give sacramental communion its meaning and its full efficacy.

We have only to remember, for example, the Last Supper, before Christ's death. How powerless the Apostles were at the Last Supper to enter into a real sensible communion with Christ's life when their faith was still inchoate, barely active, and asleep.

Now, to take a step forward, let us see the meaning of this communion in spirit through faith, and also what fosters and explains it. It is a real and efficacious communion in the paschal mystery. It is all the more important to grasp something of this because the form of contemplation proposed throughout this stage of the Exercises is its practical aspect; through this it becomes the occasion and the means of truly experiencing the Passion mysteries.

We shall proceed as follows. First of all, by reflecting on the all-embracing nature of Christ's saving act, we shall better understand the extent of its true presence and significance for all times (this is the aspect of the Passion which permeates the whole of history). After this we shall see how it is by this presence that we can make ourselves present in faith to this act of Christ. This is our presence of communion, which consists first of all in our consent to become involved in this universal, life-giving, present action before we fashion our own lives into a prolongation of this saving action of Christ, into a Church of salvation in the heart of the world.

2. The All-Embracing Nature of the Paschal Mystery

The Passion of Christ—like the whole of the paschal mystery from the Last Supper to the outpouring of the Spirit—should be considered as an act both historical and transhistorical. As an historical act this event has boundaries in space and time. It is lived by the real Christ in his flesh and his spirit, and it constitutes a precise act performed by a free person who expresses in it his commitment, love, and fidelity. In its transhistorical aspect this act gathers together everything which (throughout the whole of history—before, during, and after Jesus' life) was, is, or will be in need of salvation. From all directions history culminates in this point of time in which the act of salvation is situated. It is as though, by its roots, this act touched and penetrated, in the whole of human history and in the history of each person, everything that had need of being saved (sins, limitations, temptations, sufferings, and death), to bring it all before God and to integrate it in an infinite act of fidelity which has become in love an infinite expiation for the sin of mankind and an infinite praise rendered by man to God. Through this unique way of love, which thus includes both expiation and praise, all the perishable material of our world and of our lives has been brought before God to be transformed into an experience of life. Christ is the place in which this strange and wonderful exchange took place. Even if the lived experience of this saving operation cost an entire lifetime of obedience, it is at this hour of salvation that Christ consummated his work when, freely, without being obliged to do so, he surrendered his life for the salvation of the multitude.

3. Our Consent to the Paschal Mystery

By the fact of this all-embracing character described above, Christ's saving act takes on the expansive qualities of universality, permanence, and presence. Although it was performed in time (it is a historical act), it touched what is today an object of salvation, and what will be so tomorrow and the day after tomorrow, in my own life as in that of all created beings (it is transhistorical). So it is in regard to something already borne and expiated that I can today give my consent that this saving act be applied in my life with all its efficacy. It is possible that for many persons or for many acts Christ hung on the cross uselessly. Nevertheless, he himself consented to be there for everyone and for everything. But it is possible for me today, by my free consent to the pardon of the Father in Christ, to confer on the Savior's action its liberating efficacy for me—just as my free refusal can condemn it to futility in the same way that man did with the entire work of the Creator before salvation came.

To undergo through communion the mystery of the Passion at this stage of the retreat experience will then consist first of all in making myself present to this act. In faith I shall perceive it as having myself within it and consenting to be integrated into it so as to gather the immensely free and loving fruit of divine pardon coming from God through the suffering Christ. By following the dynamic of this experience, I shall enter more consciously into the saving act which regenerates me; and once I have done that, I shall consent to participate in the universal work of salvation which thus develops into a growing Church, the living Body of Christ which completes in his members the passion of its Head.

4. Résumé

Vatican Council II makes clear the meaning of the term "paschal mystery" within the context of God's plan of salvation: ". . . the work of Christ our Lord in redeeming mankind and giving perfect glory to God. He achieved his task principally by the paschal mystery of his blessed passion, resurrection from the dead, and glorious ascension" (On the Liturgy, nos. 5 and 6).

In the light of this, we can summarize what we have stated. To contemplate and experience the Passion means to make oneself intimately present, through a living faith, to Christ's saving act considered in its universal aspects as part of the paschal mystery. It means, further, to consent with the whole of one's being to being personally integrated into this paschal mystery, to pass into the life which Christ has destined for us, and to accept a more conscious participation in the building up of his Kingdom, which is the total Body of Christ in process of being built up. It is important to keep in mind that this act of faith, of presence in contemplation (an act which is extended and worked out in time by the contemplation of the various events of the Passion), embodies and combines the concrete material of the retreatant's own past and of his present spiritual experience. The election, now more clearly formulated and more consciously in the heart, will normally concretize this consent, this abandonment to and union with the saving Christ, and also this communion in God's plan for the whole of creation.

B. Overall Interpretation of the Chief Events of the Paschal Mystery

The principal events or "mysteries" of the paschal cycle are contemplated during the Third and Fourth Weeks taken together. I shall now treat them briefly, on a level of interpretation which situates them within the perspective proposed above—of contemplation, experience, consent, integration, and participation. I think that these mysteries should be presented to the retreatant in this perspective if one wishes to help him or her to contemplate in this manner—to make himself present to the mysteries grasped in their existential dimension indicated by faith. The method of contemplation, properly so-called, which is presence to the Gospel event with one's whole intelligent, emotional, real self, does not change. But the act of faith which directs or inspires this presence ought to be enlightened and conformed to the truths which God has revealed.

Here they invite us to pity for Christ, yes, but even more to sharing in the acts by which he bears our sins and expiates them in order to make a new life for us. He is carrying our own lives toward a genuine freedom. "Do not weep for me," said Jesus to the daughters of Jerusalem, "but weep for yourselves and for your children" (Luke 23:28).

1. The Supper: the Mystery of Salvation in Its Totality

During the Last Supper Christ lived in its entirety the whole paschal mystery in its overall significance within God's plan of salvation and brought eternal life for humankind. This makes it the high point of history, gathering together every manifestation of evil and death in order to carry them toward life by way of expiation and praise. The efficacious word accomplishes what it says; and when Jesus freely surrenders his life, he gives to mankind the divine life, the Spirit himself. Thus the Apostles, receiving his body and his blood, received this great gift of God. But their lack of awareness constituted a major obstacle to the divine action, which does not impose itself in any way on the will of man. No one is forced to enter the Kingdom of God.

Thus the Last Supper virtually contained, and continues to contain, Christ's act of offering himself, the agony which followed and delivered him over to the powers of evil, the judgment and the condemnation through which the sinful world of every age condemned the God-man; his death, resurrection, and apparitions after it; his ascension to the Father in the presence of his nascent Church; and his efficacious gift of the Spirit for this Church and its welfare in time and eternity. For two reasons, however, this entire content of the Last Supper will be extended in time. First of all, Christ himself, fully submitting to the laws of the Incarnation, will live in his flesh, to the very limit of his possibilities (even to death), this salvation experience which he as the Word Incarnate accomplished in spirit, but efficaciously, at the Last Supper. Secondly, for us this language of happenings, of visible acts performed in time and transmissible in time, helps us to understand better, or at least to conjecture, the unsearchable riches of content of this saving Last Supper, and to share in a tangible, perceptible, and social or communal way in the later celebration of this Supper and the various other events pertaining to the history of our salvation. Otherwise, in all probability, we would have been constrained to knowing and living all these realities in spirit only. This would have been the difficult portion of only a few who could understand it, and would have contradicted the constant dimensions of incarnation and sacramentalism which characterize the whole of the gratuitous and generous history of our salvation.

Presented in this way in its global significance, the mystery of the Last Supper is proposed for the retreatant's contemplation experience. The "experience" aspect consists, as is to be expected, in union attained by gazing with accepting faith on our Savior's free act of offering himself for the entire and now imminent work of salvation. It is one's own concrete life that one must here unite with Christ, and that particularly in the light of the election which makes more concrete at this point of time the retreatant's efficacious will to be conformed to his will, to live in union with him and for his Kingdom.

As for the contemplation which inspires this interior will to offer oneself in union with Christ who surrenders Himself, we can nourish it through the three principal elements in the narrative of the Last Supper in the Gospels. First, there is the washing of the feet, which expresses Christ's own interior attitude and gives us the key to the events which follow. Christ came to manifest to men and women the love which places him thus at their service. He makes himself the slave of their salvation, of the act of the most total purification which he freely offers them. Next is the paschal meal. It constitutes the heart of the mystery. Here Christ performs the symbolic actions which for more than a thousand years have been repeated by his people. They are actions which are at the same time a memorial of the deliverance coming from God, a renewal of the Covenant contract with God on Sinai, and an expression of desire for the life to come, that of the Messianic times. By celebrating this gesture so rich in significance, Jesus gives it a new and still richer meaning, that of the immediate realization of the Messianic hopes. His act creates the New Covenant of man with God, in which God gives himself to man in Jesus and in which man, in Jesus, gives a perfect response to the love of the Father. Third and finally, there is the discourse after the Supper, when Jesus explains at length what may be considered in this supreme moment as the height of his message —a message of unity in the sharing of divine life, a message of love, of peace, and of joy for the ages to come.

2. The Reading of the Passion according to the Two Chief Gospel Traditions

We now know that the sequel of the Passion makes the rich content of the Last Supper clear and helps us to communicate with it "in truth." To someone who would wish to contemplate the events of the Passion in one channel of inspiration, we might suggest the practical procedure of taking its events from one Gospel, for example, that of John.

Moreover, it is good to recognize that the events narrated in the four Gospels come from two chief traditions, which themselves have their source in the oral narratives of the Passion in the primitive Church. The first tradition was connected with the Suffering Servant in Isaiah; this made it evident that it was through suffering and death that Christ brought about the work of our salvation. The other tradition, influenced by the glorious Messiah of Daniel, placed the accent on that other aspect of the same reality, namely, that by suffering and dying Christ accomplished our salvation as a glorious work. Mark and Matthew took their inspiration from the first tradition following Isaiah, while Luke and John exemplify the second tradition, according to which the Father through the Passion glorifies his own Son.

3. The Agony: Awareness of the Sin of the World and Acceptance of Its Guilt

It has been said of Christ's agony that it was the interior aspect of the Passion. This is so, I think, because the agony shows the painful knowledge Jesus had of the immense weight of that hour when the work of salvation was consummated. After his baptism, when Jesus lined up with sinners, he was immediately led by the Spirit to come face to face with the power of the devil who was going to oppose him. But at the Last Supper Jesus pronounced a more decisive affirmation—a yes which now, in fact, delivers him over, hands and feet bound, to this unleashed power of darkness. "But this is your hour," said Jesus, "and the power of darkness" (Luke 22:53). So we can say that Christ's suffering in the agony, felt in his whole body and spirit (sadness and agony, fear and anguish, distress and sweat of blood), is much more than a psychological pain provoked by the prospect of suffering and death. It is Jesus' clear realization that he has reached that certain moment when he is carrying, in God's eyes, all the sins of the people of all time: "God made him to be sin for us" (Rom. 8:5); he is the one who takes on himself all the anger of God, who repudiates sin for all eternity.

It is then, when he is at the bottom of the abyss of evil and at close quarters with all the hatreds, blasphemies, and infidelities, it is then that Christ remains faithful, reaffirms his love for the Father and his will, and "passes over," with us who are the reason for his sacrifice and act of praise, into the love which regenerates us.

So it is in the measure of our faith and communion with this act of Christ in which we are contained, with our burden of misery, of limitation, of faults, and in proportion to our consent to being integrated into this act of love of Christ become sin in our stead, that we are drawn after him into the Father's infinite love which totally regenerates us. It is an experience, repeated for us, of baptism and of pardon in the Spirit.

In my opinion, this is the content and the interpretation of the mystery which should guide the retreatant's contemplation experience at this point.

It is to this deep reality of the interior agony of Christ that one must be present in faith; and it is to being integrated in it through one's whole life that one can consent, also in an enlightened, humble, loving faith.

4. The Trial: the World Judges and Condemns God

The incidents in the trial of Jesus are another occasion for the comprehensive or universal aspects in the mystery of the Passion. In fact, it was not the condemnatory sentence of the Jews and Romans alone that led Christ to his death. Combining everything into one moment, their trial made visible and explicit to the world the trial in which all human beings of all time judge and condemn God in the person of his Son, the God-man. By the fact that the proceedings are political and religious, including as they do the priests and the people as well as Herod and Pilate, they reveal still more the deep tendency in human beings to judge and condemn God and to cover up everything in our own lives which might be put on trial. These proceedings are the opposite of what St. Paul calls obedience arising from faith (Rom. 1:5). Likewise, in this respect, the history of human beings appears to be a constant diabolical straying. Through all their faults which contribute to an absolute self-assertion, human beings have sought to substitute themselves for every Absolute, for every Transcendence, for God himself. Our personal faults more or less consciously reproduce on their own scale the same pretension.

This is why, when we make ourselves present through faith at the trial to which Jesus was submitted, we should be aware that it is radically our own, that it runs all through history. It is our history to the degree that "the world" is alive in ourselves, for it has judged and still judges and condemns God. The trial of Jesus goes on without ever coming to an end on the world's stage and in the depths of our hearts, whether it is directed at Jesus himself and his message as distorted in various ideologies (atheism, secularism, some systems of theology), or at his living persecuted members in our poor, oppressed, discredited brethren. On all these levels we can judge and condemn in various ways by denying, betraying, abandoning, washing our hands, encouraging, or executing.

Moreover, on the occasion of this contemplation experience, it is also important to be aware that we, too, can be placed in the dock with Jesus, to the degree in which we accept being with him against the world which judges and condemns. Let us remember, then, that it is most often in ourselves that the world will judge and condemn us, in the exact measure in which we refuse any longer to associate ourselves with what is in opposition to God, his existence, his Kingdom, his demands.

5. The Death of Christ and the Scriptures

For the retreatant who enters into the mystery of Christ's death, I have no contemplation to propose which is founded on a particular theological interpretation. Elements of such a theology can be found elsewhere.[1] Instead, I prefer to suggest some reflections taken directly from the Scriptures. In this way these passages themselves become an occasion for contemplation, helping us to accept and to understand in the Spirit this supreme mystery of Christ put to death. Among other references I propose the following:

1. First of all, there is the connection of this fact with the history of evil and of our sins, which culminates in the death of Christ, source of our life. See Rom. 6:23, Luke 22:53, and Acts 3:15.

2. The Christ put to death is the well-beloved Son, rejected by his own. See Isa. 5 and Mark 17.

3. The Christ put to death is also the Suffering Servant of Yahweh who bears our sins. See Isa. 53.

4. Finally, he is the one who was pierced, whose free death on the cross, offered for his friends, reveals the ultimate secret of the life of the Father, who is love, and gives us his Spirit, who is life. See Zach. 12:9-12; 13:6; and John 19:31-37.

5. To conclude, there is the prayer Christ himself said on the cross, overcoming every form of despair with the expression of his unshakable confidence in the Father. See Psalm 22.

6. The Resurrection: The New Life Offered to Creation and to Humankind

The meaning of the Fourth Week of the Exercises, which begins with the resurrection of Christ, is clear if we refer to the fruit for which Ignatius makes us ask during this stage: to enter into the joy of the Risen Christ. As I have explained more fully elsewhere,[2] this is not a question of a simple psychological joy (any more than the sorrow and agony of Christ was no more than simply psychological), like the joy of a convalescent person who is returning to health or of one who has happily concluded a difficult task. In other words, Jesus' joy is not about himself. Rather, his joy, which is essentially apostolic, is about the Kingdom accomplished on this day, about the new life transmitted to the entire world, that has finally become capable, in principle at least, of accepting it and of communicating with God. Hence, it is the joy of the love of the Spouse welcoming the

---

1 For example, in *Lumière et Vie*, no. 101 (March 1971), devoted to the death of Christ.
2 *Biblical Theology and the Spiritual Exercises*, pp. 304-307.

bride who has become capable of responding, at this point of time, to the love which from all eternity has been waiting for her in the heart of God.

This life offered to the whole of creation, which will progressively enter into possession of this gift of God by a free response to Love, was able to find immediate acceptance only in Mary, the only creature whose journey through life needed no subsequent purification and whose faith, matured at the foot of the cross, was simply an expectation of the total completion of the work of redemption. As we shall see, the other disciples had to feel their way step by step, according to their slowly growing belief, towards that full acceptance of Christ as truly alive again. This is what the other apparitions will show us.

To enter into the joy of the Risen Christ is then, first of all, to be present to that total victory of life and of love in Jesus, and to the embrace between him and regenerated humanity—a humanity accepted by him in spirit in its totality, and already contacted in the person of Mary, the link willed by God from the beginning between consenting humanity and the coming of its Lord. Further, to enter into the joy of the Risen Christ is also for the retreatant to perceive himself or herself bathed in the rays of Christ's joy. For this vision extends to this person in particular, who exists, willed by God, in this project of life, and is one of the long line of the faithful on pilgrimage, since that day, towards the living heart of the Lord.

7. The Apparitions: Appropriation of the Fruit of the Resurrection

The apparitions should not be reduced to the objective phenomenon of Christ making himself visible to certain persons. They are above all the expression of an advance along the road of that faith which gradually accepts Christ as living, and participates in the deliverance which the Risen Christ brings along with himself. In fact, Christ did not appear to anyone of those who did not have faith. To the others he showed himself sooner or later, according to the lessening of their resistances and the maturation of their faith: to Magdalen, to the holy women, to Peter, to the disciples of Emmaus, to the group of apostles, to Thomas. Therefore the apparitions constitute personal experience, in faith, of the living Christ who is no longer to be sought among the dead. This experience necessarily accompanies deliverance from the manifestations of evil which have hitherto hindered one from total surrender to Christ, to love, and to eternal life.

Why, then, and how do we contemplate the apparitions? First, because they are the appropriation by personal witnesses of that grace which the Lord destines for all believers. This spiritual experience is expressed here through the desire to enter into the joy of the Risen Lord. This experience of witnesses, besides revealing the characteristics which should be the aim of our own experience, is also its foundation and opens the way to it. Our own faith experience, which is fundamentally concerned here, cannot be accomplished in isolation, without communication with that of our predecessors, especially those whom the Spirit has brought into view for our guidance.

Secondly, it seems less good for us to contemplate these apparitions from the viewpoint of those who are experiencing them. There might be a risk of identifying with one or other of them and then of shutting ourselves up in a short-lived psychologism. Let us recall certain notes of Ignatius for this period: to ask to enter into the joy of the Risen Lord during this entire stage, and to see how Jesus consoled those to whom he appeared. Hence, it is always from the viewpoint of Christ that we should do our contemplating during the Fourth Week. It is important to stop and see how he confirms each one in his faith, delivering him or her from his special evil and inviting him to share in that freedom, life, light, joy, and eternal youth that he himself has become.

By dint of looking at Christ in what he has become for himself and for others, the retreatant will be able, in turn and as the result of patient acts of presence, to accept the ever-living Christ in a personal way; he will be able to understand that, united to him, he will always be delivered from evil, capable of going forward in this light of life where his Lord has gone before him. In this way his experience will be one of appropriation of the same fruit of the resurrection, the apparition of the Risen Lord ever present in his life of faith.

Finally, the exercises might in practice be centered on the apparitions as they are narrated in the Gospels and in the Acts of the Apostles— down to the apparition to St. Paul, as Ignatius specifies in the Exercises ([310]). In them the retreatant will see how Magdalen is freed from her despair; Peter, from his remorse and guilty conscience; the disciples of Emmaus, from their spiritual pessimism; Thomas, from his doubt and his hardness. We also see how each one is renewed in life, in love, and in commitment to the following of Christ. Since all Christians are invited to this, they will carry their cross. This is essentially a sharing, in this life, in Christ's Passion, which is the passage towards life; but they will do this in that light which those who follow in his footsteps know.

8. The Ascension: Return to the Universal—Spirit and Mission

St. Ignatius leads his retreatant as far as the mystery of the Ascension and leaves him there—left, he hopes, to the Holy Spirit, who involves him and guides him in the universal mission manifested in its essence by this last mystery in Christ's own self-revealing.

The Ascension is the "return to the Father," in the words of St. John (16:5-13; 17). The moment has now come for Christ to make his presence burst forth beyond the limits of space and time. He reveals the universal dimension of his mission to his disciples, calling them to open themselves through and in the Spirit, who inaugurates his new presence to the world.

As for the retreatant who, like the Apostles, has reread Christ's message in the light of post-Resurrection faith, he or she has been sensitized to this dimension of the Kingdom from the first meditations on it. But once he arrives in some way at the summit of this process of very intimate assimilation, of appropriation to himself of the saving act of Christ, in his turn he is brought back, by way of the contemplation experience, to the universal character of the Kingdom, to the mission which the "departure" of Christ has brought out more clearly. Through Christ, the Head of the new Body which is creation, humanity is oriented in this direction of ascension and light towards the Father; and the world itself ought to be built up continually in this same direction.

Henceforth this hope will indefectibly sustain the believer's commitment, founded on the solid rock of Christ. The Ascension, the last mystery of Christ as visible among us, remains the living indicative sign to which the mission is a response. It is a being sent forth to the humble, daily task of building up the Body in the Spirit, this Body which is the Church, the whole Christ living in the midst of the world. "And while they were gazing into heaven as he went, behold, two men stood by them in white robes, and said, 'Men of Galilee, why do you stand looking into heaven?'" Jesus had left them as his last message: "You shall be my witnesses in Jerusalem and in all Judea and Samaria and to the end of the earth" (Acts 1:10-11, and 8).

C. The Spiritual Fruits of This Stage

The stage we have just gone through, the last of the six stages envisaged at the end of chapter 2, comprises a fairly large portion of the experience (the Third and Fourth Weeks of the Exercises). It is rich in content (the whole paschal mystery, from the Last Supper to the beginnings of the Church) and rather complex in structure (carried out by the way of a contemplation experience). As a help in following the work on the strictly subjective level, I shall summarize the objectives which have been pursued on this level. I shall do this by examining three principal fruits which have been aimed at and whose progressive and relative appearance in the retreatant's experience has been a help to see the way clearly and to assure the continuation of the work.

The first fruit results from the retreatant's consent, by means of contemplation in faith, to become integrated into the universal action of Christ our Savior during this Third Week. This fruit is one of liberation with regard to one's own death, which in reality acquires the character of a way to life. In this way, as I mentioned above, the man or woman of enlightened faith remains a participant in the Passion of Christ through his or her whole life. Carrying the cross faithfully in the steps of the Master, he or she can no longer live the Passion in darkness, but in the light of life which is known by anyone who really follows Christ.

The second fruit is of the same order: deliverance from evil. But here it becomes linked to the retreatant's immediate, day-by-day life. This fruit of the Fourth Week follows from the experience of entering into the joy of the Risen Lord. Through this experience the retreatant sees himself, in a certain sense, as a source of Christ's joy, by discovering himself as being loved by Him, participating in the life he rejoices to give by joining every human being to the Father and to his love. This fruit becomes the consciousness of being freed from evil in the measure of this union with Christ, and a confirmation of the way taken, which concretizes the foundational election, that form of the "more" or "greater" which Christ and the Spirit call for and assure in our life.

Finally, the last important fruit results from the final section of the Exercises, the mystery of the Ascension, which ushers in the transition into mission in the Church as seen in the Acts of the Apostles and even in the retreatant's very own life. It is an intense fruit of commitment in the Spirit to a dynamic incorporation into the Church and the service of the Kingdom. This last point, which is wide open to the future, constitutes what is perhaps the most precious overall fruit of the entire experience of the Exercises. It is so important that I shall develop it more fully in the following chapter. I mean the precise fruit which, with St. Paul, I shall call "life in the Spirit."

D. Suggestions for Readings on the Third and Fourth Weeks

Besides the material pertinent to these Weeks which is furnished in the Biblical Bibliography of my *Biblical Theology and the Spiritual Exercises*, pages 361-364, I here suggest some readings which might be used directly by the retreatant in the course of the preceding contemplations.

1. On the Last Supper: David Stanley, *Modern Scriptural Approach*, chs. 21 to 24, pp. 212-241; also Jean Laplace, *Experience of Life in the Spirit*, pp. 123-128.

2. On the Passion (in general): D. Stanley, *Modern Scriptural Approach*, ch. 26, pp. 250-262; J. Laplace, *Experience of Life*, pp. 145-155; Hans Urs von Balthasar, *Heart of the World*, ch. 5, pp. 91-103; *Lumière et Vie*, no. 101 (1971), "La mort du Christ."

3. On the Agony: D. Stanley, *Modern Scriptural Approach*, ch. 25, pp. 242-249; Von Balthasar, *Heart of the World*, ch. 6, pp. 104-132.

4. On the Trial: *Lumière et Vie*, as in fn. 2 above.

5. On the Death of Christ, von Balthasar, *Heart of the World*, ch. 9, pp. 145-153; *Ledrus*, Meditations 42 and 43, "Face au crucifix" and "Le trépas du Fils de l'homme"; *Lumière et Vie*, as in fn. 2 above.

6. On the Resurrection and Ascension: J. Laplace, *Experience of Life*, pp. 166-178.

7. On the Joy of the Risen Christ: von Balthasar, *Heart of the World*, ch. 10, pp. 157-173.

8. On the Apparitions: to Magdalen: ibid., pp. 158-163; to Thomas: ibid., pp. 163-165; to Peter at Tiberias: ibid., pp. 162-163.

9. On the Ascension: ibid., pp. 171-173; 181-183.

On Christ in relation to the Resurrection, Ascension, and mission in the Spirit and the Church, see D. Stanley, *Modern Scriptural Approach*, chs. 24 and 30, pp. 288-306. Several chapters of R. Guardini, *The Lord*, can also be useful. Finally, among the commentaries, I recommend the article by F. X. Durrwell, "Mystère pascal et Parousie," *Nouvelle Revue Théologique*, 95 (1973), pp. 253-278 (especially the second part, pp. 266-278).

PART III

PROLONGATIONS
OF THE EXPERIENCE OF THE EXERCISES

Chapter 10

LIFE IN THE SPIRIT
AFTER THE EXERCISES HAVE ENDED

A. The Exercises as an Apprenticeship to Life in the Spirit

Life in the Spirit seems to be the most normal result of the intensive experience of making the Exercises, whether they are made in the seclusion of a closed retreat or in everyday life. In fact, a capital function of the Exercises has consisted in fostering special efforts toward a better-structured and nourished spiritual life after the exercises as a course have been completed. Because of this they are a kind of education for life in the Spirit,[1] on both the subjective level of the retreatant's interior life and on the objective level of their content, which nourishes it.

On the objective level of the thought presented in the *Exercises*, the retreatant has been progressively contemplating in the Spirit God's plan for the creation, redemption, spiritual growth, and eventual glorification of the men and women who freely cooperate with his plan. This saving plan, which runs through the whole Bible and unifies all its books, is concerned with the action of the Father and the Son in the world and in human beings. The retreatant's entire personal history, past and present, has revealed the active presence of the Spirit. For this particular person, the Exercises have been a work of Pentecost, that is, a progressive insertion into the movement of the Spirit acting in our time, a more total grasp of the Spirit on the life of this person who has surrendered to God in the past and is striving to take his or her part in furthering God's plan unfolding in the history of salvation.

---

1   We glimpse the meaning of life in the spirit from descriptions in St. Paul: "I say then, walk by the Spirit and you will not gratify the desire of the flesh. . . . If you are guided by the Spirit. . . . If you are led by the Spirit, [you will not do the works of the flesh]. . . . But in contrast, the fruit of the Spirit is love, joy, peace, patience, kindness, generosity, faithfulness, gentleness, self-control. . . . If we live in the Spirit, let us also follow the Spirit" (Gal. 5:16-25. See also 1 Cor. 10:31).

From the Principle and Foundation onward, with the help of the objective formulation of the unifying vision arising from Christian faith the retreatant has become progressively more aware of God's revelation in his or her life. That history of personal faith, of progressive appropriation of the work of salvation in one's life, has helped in the recognition of God present and active throughout one's concrete existence from the first years of conscious life down to the present day. In its way, this was already the work of the Spirit hovering over the chaos of a new genesis (see Genesis 1:1-2, 27).

In the First Week, with the history of personal sins, we have done more than examine our conscience in regard to a situation of sin and spiritual poverty. These limitations which we have felt as active in our lives have, by the light of faith, taken on the aspect of special occasions to experience the saving love of God and the call to a unique ascent, namely, to a total "life in Him."

This is why the retreatant's personal history was again taken up in a positive way, when she or he considered the Kingdom with a view to discerning, through the dynamics operative in his own self, the possibilities already emerging for a more radical offering of self to "life in Christ," the only way to eternal life. This too was the purpose of the next series of Exercises, by means of a progressively more personal work of discernment carried into such detail that no possibility of self-oblation in the following of Christ was neglected. At the time of the election this following of Christ was brought into formulation, under the motions or impulses sent by the Holy Spirit, with the clear intention of entering as fully as possible into communion with the paschal mystery.

The Exercises have drawn us gradually into this life of active and committed union in absolute fidelity to the Spirit of holiness, who brings about conformity of our will with God's will. Their obvious aim was not to achieve this goal, this point of convergence, in the hope that as time passed we would be able to hold on to it as a sum of acquired capital. On the contrary, the aim of the Exercises was only to be a period of careful, organized apprenticeship opening the way to the Light, to freeing one to the action of the Spirit, in such a way that, as time passes, one continuously reinvents one's personal history within the combined history of God and humanity which continues on. It must all be continually renewed and pursued by fresh beginnings. Hardly begun, this quickening regime of the Spirit (which is precisely that of a Christian fully alive) has need of all the enthusiasm of the initial retreat experience if it is to grow still more in fidelity and conformity. Moreover, in order that this influence of the Spirit may increase in our life, from our distant past until this present moment of greater awareness which looks to the future, the initiation into recognition of the Spirit's action must be well begun and in some way brought to completion with a view to the future. The Exercises in daily life have doubtless brought this education more directly into contact with the reality of life, and the suggestions which will follow may easily have been encountered along the way. But for the director and retreatant, it is good to come back to these counsels before the intensively lived period of accompaniment comes to its end.

If the Exercises are a Pentecostal experience, Pentecost itself is their point of departure. After having received the Spirit, the Apostles had to live in the Spirit. Hence, in the rest of this chapter I shall attempt to describe what is meant by living in the Spirit, and I shall point out certain guidelines for this life in the Spirit.

B. The Regime of the Holy Spirit

The regime of the Spirit[2] is founded on "the obedience of faith" (Rom. 1:5) and is its most direct consequence.

In the Epistle to the Romans St. Paul speaks twice of this obedience which arises from faith. In 16:25-26 he writes that the hidden mysteries of Christ have been revealed "to all nations" to bring human beings the obedience of faith. It is in consequence of that revelation and of its aim that he himself has been chosen. At the beginning of this letter (1:5), he declares that he received the grace and the apostolate to preach the obedience which springs from faith.

By the obedience of faith we accept God in our life and submit ourselves to his transcendence. He expressed his power and love for us in his plan and work of creation, of redemption after the fall, and of salvation; and this latter work is continued in his active work of sanctification, the culmination of all the preceding along one simple line of ascent toward our glorification in the beatific vision. Through our free correspondence with the action of the living Spirit of the Father and Son, the work of sanctifying us on earth becomes our appropriation of his life-giving activity, which includes and accomplishes it all: creation, salvation, and glorification for eternity.

Based in this way upon the determinative (but not constraining) action of God, life in the Spirit becomes an attention to the innumerable signs from God, to the expressions of his desires as personalized to myself and

---

2 On this subject see Stanley, *Modern Scriptural Approach,* "The Law of the Spirit of Life in Christ Jesus," ch. 31, pp. 307-314, a commentary on Rom. 8:1-14.

guiding my life toward its fulfillment.

The experience of making the Exercises will teach us, at length and in detail, the foundations of a faith which finds expression in an effort at fidelity to God through submission to his Holy Spirit. This Spirit works to make us more conformed to the Son, the Unique One, the Beloved. The experience likewise makes us sensitive to the complex discernment of the action of the Spirit, which must be distinguished from the different interior motions in the soul which agitate us and must be read in the concrete context of our past and present life.

To gather together all these coordinated factors characteristic of a life in the Spirit, which is constantly guided by obedience of faith (or in other words, obedience to God's desires and invitations), I would like to devote these concluding reflections to life in the Spirit considered as an engagement to prolong the spiritual experience of the retreat into everyday life for all our remaining days. While making the Exercises, we learned to recognize God's action, the Holy Spirit's signals within us both in our past history and in our experiences as retreatants. Furthermore, we have witnessed the past and present proclamation of the word, God's revealed message, within the continuing history of salvation. Still further, during the election we have experienced our own committing of our future to the Holy Spirit acting within us. What conclusions can we draw from all this for the prolongation of the experience? What ought to be added to obtain a more complete vision of "life in the Spirit," at the heart of our lives, which we desire to be lives of fidelity?

C. Some Requirements for Life in the Spirit

Here I could be content simply to enumerate the principal conditions of life in the Spirit, which are charity, prayer, obedience, and spiritual discernment. All are necessary, with each supposing or evoking the others. But let us see briefly how they are related to the aim we have in view.

1. Charity

The first requirement is charity, since the Spirit of God is essentially a spirit of love; and we cannot "grieve" him (Eph. 4:30) without our losing the fruit of his presence and action. Moreover, it is proper to this Spirit to "pour" God's love into our hearts (Rom. 5:5), to bring us into harmony with the demands of faith whose normal expression, if it is genuine, is love (see the First Letter of St. John), interior and exterior acts of love and commitment (2 Cor. 6:6).

128

Anyone who separates himself or herself from love in his heart—the love that pardons, accepts, freely gives itself; the love that serves, refrains from judging, is not arrogant, does not pass away (1 Cor. 13:4ff)—any such person as this could not pretend to surrender to the Spirit and live by him. Neither would that person be capable of hearing the Spirit's whispered "sighs too deep for words" (Rom. 8:26), which have the power of binding a weak human person to the eternity of God. It would be quite vain to pretend that we were living by the Spirit and being intimately moved by him if charity, which is the sign of his presence, does not have the first place in our lives.[3]

2. Prayer

Prayer is not being considered here merely as a normal expression of our relationship with God and of our way of living that relationship—but even this statement affirms the absolute necessity of prayer for the prolongation of the spiritual experience of the retreat in our life. But beyond that, it does have a strict connection with the precise object of our reflection here: learning how to live by the Spirit and how to perceive his action in our daily life.

Continual effort is required to prevent the discernment of the Spirit in our life from being reduced purely to a "prudent" discernment and thus, in the last analysis, to a search based on merely human judgment. To make sure that it may be truly a spiritual discernment, a meeting with the Spirit and submission to the interior motions[4] ([313]) which he produces in our soul, it is of primary importance that our interpretation of these interior signs, and also those that are exterior, be situated within a context of prayer.

But I should like to stress especially the breadth of this concept of prayer at the end of an experience like that of the Exercises made in everyday life. It often happens that some persons who have not succeeded in integrating action and contemplation, place apostolic action and the practice of charity in opposition to forms of prayer properly so called. I do not believe that this constitutes a difficulty for the person who has learned to live in God in all things, to seek him in them and by means of them, to meet him and serve him in everything, to be with him in everything. Here

---

3 I shall return to this subject at greater length, from the same viewpoint of the prolongation of the spiritual experience of the retreat, when I speak of the Contemplation to Attain Love in the following chapter.

4 See also *SpEx*, [6, 227, 317, 330], and Ignatius' *Constitutions of the Society of Jesus*, trans. G. E. Ganss, S.J., [92] with fn. 18, [144], and [627] with fn. 6.

there is constant union, more or less explicit, which progressively creates an attitude or "state of prayer." This state, which is far from being passive, overflows with a desire to meet God in himself, a desire which can only find some satisfaction in times of prayer, personal and communitarian. This face-to-face encounter in times of quiet is absolutely indispensable to life, love, friendship. A person who lives in this interior climate of union and prayer will be sensitive to the signs of the Spirit. His or her entire life will be under the control and influence of the Spirit. If this may possibly entail the death of a certain spirit of calculation fostered by any form of legalism applied to formal prayer, it is in no way the death of prayer itself, even of formal prayer. For prayer gains in liberty and depth for the greater good of the one who prays, humbly conscious of his or her smallness and poverty and entirely dependent on God.

In regard to the exterior forms of prayer, I should like to add that, in the relation of prayer and charity between God and man, this basic prayer in faith not only underlies and nourishes other spiritual activities, but also finds its normal expression in penitential and eucharistic community liturgies, in prayer meetings, in all forms of prayer common within the Church. In other words, to assure the avoidance of any kind of formalism without sacrificing exterior forms of prayer, the Foundational prayer of faith should animate every other form of prayer and give meaning, depth, and radiance to the varied things in which it is incarnated.

3. Obedience

With St. Paul we have seen that obedience of faith is the foundation of life in the Spirit and, further, is expressed by our living in the Spirit. This means that the seeking for the Spirit, in the life of the believer, necessarily passes through this way of obedience of faith. In submitting to God through this obedience, the believer accepts God's ways coming to him directly or through the intermediaries he has chosen. Not only the existence of God, the transcendence or quality of his being, but also his revelation and his continual action—past, present, and future—become for me occasions of decision. In the history of my own life, this revelation and action of God come to my receptive self through a series of intermediaries which guide my obedience in faith—God's revealed and enlightening word; his sanctifying Spirit and his activity; and the Church, sacrament of God and of his salvation, with its own life, laws, sacraments, official interpreters, and dynamic groups. These are all just so many occasions for decisions. Through them God's directives come to me, and through them I shall learn in faith to seek, respect, and interpret in order to progress along the road of an incarnated obedience of faith.

For the religious committed by consecration to a group officially recognized by the Church, the channels of communication, of expression of the transcendence and the will of God, are quite simply multiplied and amplified to the point where they touch the details of his or her life and place it more completely within the obedience of faith through the religious obedience. To the determining structures valid for the believer within the Church are added those of the institute chosen, of its ecclesial mission, its particular spirit, its mystique, its spirituality, its rules, life, leaders, and living communities.

To live by the Spirit is to obey in faith all the liberating determinations of God in our life. It is not certain that we have known how in all instances to read and rightly interpret this liberating action of the Lord, which comes to us through these many interior, exterior, and institutional intermediaries, in such a way that we submit ourselves to this action as it comes to us through the more or less adequate signs in which it is incarnated. Life in the Spirit gives value both to religious obedience and to the obedience of faith; it restores to each its true function: to unite us to God and to make us live in him. This is, of course, on condition that those who govern do so spiritually, that is, in the Spirit, in the service of the Spirit and of liberation of the person in God.

4. Spiritual Discernment

To obey in faith, to allow ourselves to be guided by the Spirit in the realities of our life where many different determining influences mingle, requires a spirit of attention to the Spirit's motions and inspirations, a capacity to read these signs of his action. This presupposes the habit of spiritual discernment.

In the first place, we may say that the person who wishes to live by the Spirit must learn to recognize the Spirit's action in the many interior, exterior, universal, and particular signs through which he makes his good pleasure and invitations clear—personalized to ourselves—and adjusted to harmonize with the circumstances of our own lives. When we accept them, we do so to our own benefit. But we must learn how to distinguish between those which are his and those which may come from some other source.

There are first of all the universal signs which the Spirit uses and brings to our attention as time goes along, thus personalizing them to ourselves, my own self. These comprise the broad history of salvation, which has its own dynamic revealed to us by the Scriptures, by the natural process of the evolution of the world, by the history of the society of which we are a part, and by the events characteristic of our era in the Church and in society.

The Spirit is the first to act within this continuity and reality of space and time to which we belong. He sometimes turns these demands into "signs" for each of us.

Perhaps more important than this, because closer and more significant, are the signs particular to the person concerned, myself. The Spirit takes them into account in his respectful action. So we must learn to recognize these signs in one's previous experiences, in one's present psychological makeup, and in the dynamics of one's immediate sociological milieu (of life, work, and various relationships)—in short, in the reality of one's personal history, which directly includes one's spiritual experiences in faith, one's acceptance of Christ, of his revealed word, and of motions from the Spirit.

To recognize the Spirit in my life which is surrendered to his action, or in the lives of persons whom I am accompanying through the Exercises, is to take into account these different sets of circumstances which the Spirit himself respects and by means of which he communicates with and inspires this particular person, myself, for the sake of my growth in the faith.

However, as is well known, there are times and circumstances when recognition of the Spirit in the interior actions he inspires requires a more precise discernment, that is, careful appraisal to separate the truly good from the bad, or the better from the less good. For this purpose we have directives like those which St. Ignatius left us. These "rules" concern the particular times when, among the different interior motions, impulses, urges, and the like, we should try to distinguish those which are truly from God from those which may come from another source, such as Satan or merely my own self-willed desires (*SpEx*, [313-336] and [169-189]). Here I shall mention only two criteria which are of capital importance among all these rules for moments of precise discernment when the analysis of the interior motions is ordered to decisions to be made. The first is the state of peace which one of the different proposed solutions brings. The absence of peace is itself significant; but complete peace is itself matter for discernment: as to its source, its stability, its permanence, and the reality of its fruits. For it could come from a deception by the evil spirit. The rules of St. Ignatius are useful for these particular times when discernment must be exercised on various states of soul which we experience, on the interior "motions," those inclinations, impulses, thoughts, or lights which either truly lead us to God or which sooner or later separate us from him.[5]

5   For a brief and clear commentary on the Ignatian rules of discernment, I suggest the reading of lessons 25 and 25 (2) of C. A. Bernard in *Corso*, "Le discernement des esprits" and "L'interprétation des motions spirituelles." [See also H. Coathalem, *Ignatian Insights: A Guide to the Spiritual Exercises* (Taipei, 1971), pp.

But a second, highly important criterion is the one which Ignatius habitually employed in reaching decisions throughout his life: Among options, which one is most likely to lead to greater praise or glory to God? (Incidentally, this "greater glory of God" is tightly linked to the greater service of God, and it will also lead to our own greater self-fulfillment and happiness in the long run.) Ignatius indicated this criterion as the climax of his Principle and Foundation ([23]): Which of two options is more likely to be conducive to the end for which God created me? He repeats it ([179, 183, 189]) as an exercitant's chief guide during a period of election and again (under the name of service) in his Constitutions of the Society of Jesus ([622, a]), as the fundamental criterion for choosing one ministry rather than another.

Finally, for the more ordinary conduct of our life, outside the precise times of scrutiny of the interior motions of the Spirit, there is a threefold principle of the Spirit's action which it is well to bear in mind. It helps us to correspond more readily and more radically, in everything, to this control exerted by God over our life in the Spirit. I would even say that, if we guide ourselves habitually by this triple principle, we will be in a state of self-surrender to the influence of the Holy Spirit, who leads us to the Father.

First, the Spirit always builds upon what he has already begun in us. That is why we should often refer to his past action in our life, to understand his direction in the present, where it is sometimes difficult to discern. Second, it happens that his action is sometimes continued through ruptures, uprootings, or sudden changes of direction which seem to indicate a certain lack of continuity in ideas. By reference to the past, and to the apparent breaks in it, the uprootings in the present can often reveal to us deep continuities in our life along a journey which we never suspected. Third, it is always for our good that the Spirit acts, demands, tries, or consoles—for the well-being of our filial growth, in Christ, towards the Father, in the saving Church.

By its being based on the obedience of faith, and by discernment of the action and the control of God on our existence, life in the Spirit thus becomes the context in which we spontaneously raise the question about the prolongation, after the retreat has ended, of the spiritual experience which the retreatant had during this period of intensive application. At the end of the experience almost every retreatant asks: How can this be done

243-278. For a thorough study see J. Toner, *A Commentary on St Ignatius' Rules for the Discernment of Spirits: A Guide to the Principles and Practice* (St Louis, 1982). Editor.]

in our everyday life? In our next chapter we shall see, in this context of commitment and fidelity, several solutions offered for our initiative, as varied as they are complementary.

Chapter 11

PROLONGATIONS OF THE RETREAT EXPERIENCE IN A PERSONALIZED MANNER

There are, no doubt, many ways of repeating or continuing, in one's personal spiritual life, the spiritual experience which reaches its completion with the close of the Exercises made in everyday life. When I am asked about this, I usually suggest three possibilities: (1) the simple repetition of the experience with certain modifications; (2) a repetition based on the points which reveal the circularity of the Christian experience; (3) finally, St. Ignatius' own suggestion in the Contemplation to Attain Love for God. This closing contemplation is eminently fit to nourish a dedicated spiritual commitment for a time indefinitely long.

A. The Simple Repetition of the Experience

Several times it has happened that, when the retreatant had finished the intensive experience of the Exercises, he or she felt a strong desire to repeat it by himself so as to spread it over a longer period of time at a slower pace, to pray it more, and learn to let it penetrate more deeply into his life. This is a very simple way of profiting from a past experience which has evidently not yet borne all the fruit it can.

To this end I think that the person concerned should have at his or her disposal all the necessary material to proceed by himself—the Bible and suitable biblical references, commentaries on the Exercises, and especially personal notes taken during the course of the preceding experience. Referring back to the Ignatian principle of repetition, I then insist that the retreatant spend time principally on what has helped him most in the past, on what helped to produce the greatest fruit.

As to the accompaniment during the course of this repetition, it is evident that it will be much less regular, perhaps even nonexistent. However, it is always good as far as possible to have recourse from time to time to the good offices of a friend, a counselor, a confessor to see where we are and to make sure of a better discernment at the more intense moments of the experience.

Within this context of an experience in which the person is more "on his or her own," and which is geared above all to the normal rhythm of the person's life, the liturgy can play a considerable part each day with its proper cycle embracing the same line of development and assimilation of the mysteries of salvation.

B. The Circularity of the Experience

The experience we have been living during a whole year did not develop in a manner exclusively linear. The retreatant will have been struck by the fact that the fundamental vision of the beginning kept on coming back as the basis of all the other stages of the experience. Likewise, the stage in our section I of the road which we covered in three stages (1) started by deepening our hold on this outlook arising from faith, (2) next viewed the place of evil in God's plan of salvation and its history, and (3) finally concentrated on Christ our Savior. After that, section II, the stage of assimilation with its three stages dictated by the dynamic of the revelation contained in the four Gospels, was never outside the orbit of this vision. Instead the vision was further deepened through its focus on Jesus' going through his passion, death, and resurrection, the paschal mystery through which he brought God's plan to its full realization.

Consequently, it appears more clearly at the end that all the six stages interpenetrate one another. In order that the "yes" of the final stage, this consent given to the mystery of death and resurrection in union with Christ, may be possible, it is absolutely necessary that all the previous stages remain something present and fully alive in the person's experience here and now. This is the circularity of the Christian experience as we have analyzed it. It corresponds analogically to the three "ways" or stages of the spiritual life. In fact, St. Teresa says that the unitive way could never be possible unless at the same time the exigencies of the purgative and illuminative ways were repeated and assured within it. St. Paul wisely puts us on our guard when he writes: "Therefore let any one who thinks that he stands take heed lest he fall" (1 Cor. 10:12). For our part, we must assure that totality of the experience which expresses itself in that "yes" of the final stage. This vigorous affirmation constitutes that culmination of the retreat experience—just as much as does its modest implementation in our daily lives.

From the foregoing we may conclude that the spontaneity of this "yes" terminating the retreat becomes the criterion of the vitality of all the stages previously experienced. In order that this assent may be possible and efficacious, it must contain the vitality of the vision of faith, the purification which makes the commitment a free act, and the commitment itself constantly being renewed through listening to the Word Incarnate, all this under the impelling graces of the Holy Spirit. On the contrary, if our daily assent to the mystery of death and resurrection in Christ is hesitant, poor, purposeless, it becomes a sign for us of deficiency in the experience and calls for a renewal of the basics necessary for its vitality.

Hence, if we are existentially aware of this fact of the circularity of the spiritual experience—of its living totality at the moment of its consummation—we have these very dynamic criteria for its verification. These criteria will enable us quickly to discern the points of weakness in our interior journey. It will then be easy to see where efforts must be made for the desired prolongation of the experience we have been living—a renewal and a deepening of the fundamental vision of faith; an intensification of the process of purification and liberation from evil in Christ our Savior; a more intimate renewal of that friendship with Christ which will be strengthened by a long familiarity with the Gospels; a better recognition of the present inspirations of the Lord, under the guidance of the Spirit; and a more existential acceptance of the real content of that paschal mystery which Christ invites us to share.

It should be noted that the same criteria can help us to decide objectives for individual annual retreats. In them we can concentrate on particular points with a view to revitalizing, continuing, and deepening the whole experience.

C. The Contemplation to Increase Our Love for God

The final suggestion I shall make, and not by any means the least, is what St. Ignatius proposes at the end of the Exercises. We know that, when retreatants made only the First Week and stopped their experience there, he asked that practical advice be given to help them to be faithful to the new practices—instructing them in methods of praying and making examinations of conscience, urging them to greater frequency of confession and communion, and so forth. Ignatius similarly ends the course of the Exercises by a very helpful suggestion for the prolongation of the experience, but it bears less on the ways of praying which have now been acquired by practice, than on one specific element of the retreat experience. Here we are referring to his Contemplation to Attain Love. In my opinion, this contemplation constitutes a way of repeating and prolonging the lived experience in a manner which makes the theological line of the *Exercises* clear and invites us to nourish ourselves directly by them.

In fact, the whole experience of the Exercises will have consisted in making the content of the faith progressively more explicit through its application to our own life. This opens up, through growing faith, hope, love, and attachment, an experience of personal commitment strictly conditioned by a "discreet charity," this love which is measured out by God himself, through the influence of his Spirit in the soul of the believer.

This is the path Ignatius invites us to take directly, at the end of the experience of the Exercises, in order that we may live by it then and on into our daily existence. What faith has awakened during this privileged period of time is the awareness of a committed love on the part of God; and this calls for a return of love on our part—a love fully committed and surrendered to the divine will. Here we find again the two preliminary notes of the Ignatian contemplation on love which creates reciprocity and is proved by deeds ([230-231]). The love of God, discerned in the reality of everyday life, calls forth a return of love which will be expressed in service of the Lord. The only difference between it and the experience of the Exercises, I should say, is that here we find a more explicit illumination of the same road. The grace to be asked for in the Ignatian contemplation is precisely "in all things to love and serve His Divine Majesty" ([233]).

But since dialectical interactions between faith and love constitute the experience, the same interactions will be used in this exercise to perceive in all things the goodness and love of God (this is reading them from the viewpoint of faith), so that, in a movement of gratitude, I may be able in all things to love and serve His Divine Majesty ([233]). In other words, we accustom ourselves, with an active and attentive faith, to recognize in all things the love of God manifesting itself with prodigality; and we do this in order to learn to respond to this love in every circumstance, by a love of our own which is also total: "Take, O Lord, and receive all my liberty" ([234]).

On this basic dialectical interaction of gifts seen in faith and gratitude begetting love, Ignatius proposes the four points of his contemplation. They are four open paths to the contemplation which, practically speaking, is a deepening of this one same faith interpretation to which our contemplative prayer leads us. The fruits of progress in love will spontaneously emerge as a result of this dialectical procedure, once it has been experienced.

Let us say briefly that the first step in this interpretation from faith includes in one embrace all the gifts we receive from God on every level, of every kind: material and spiritual, universal and particular. These gifts are immense, multiple, varied, and polyvalent. One could enlarge on all this, but I shall not do so. It is, however, a good thing to help the believer at the outset to exercise his spirit of faith.

The second point or step in this interpretation is that which concerns God's very essence, his diffusive goodness by which he reveals himself through his gifts. These are by no means anonymous; they speak a language, that of a benevolent presence and of an infinite love which gives itself.

A third way in which to exercise our contemplation is to see how God conducts himself as one who is laboring in the multiple gifts he makes of all things and of himself. These gifts are living expressions of an unfolding love story revealing unsuspected dimensions.

Finally, at the summit of this ascending recognition in faith, and at the heart of this growing familiarity with God by which we find him in all things, we come to the point of ultimate union, perhaps a union of a mystical order, of union with God on the occasion of anything or every-thing. At this point, every creature becomes the occasion of a closer encounter with God—a kind of springboard by which we can reach God's very being, the unique source of all these beings which, each in its own way, express and radiate the Infinity of God translated into creation.

This road of reading creatures from the viewpoint of faith, of growth in love attracted to an intense deepening of relations, should not be reduced simply to the matter of "making a meditation." It is a vital way of contemplation to which the experience of the Exercises serves merely as an initiation; and we should be aware of this fact. The retreatant can opt in full lucidity for this simple daily practice which encourages growth in finding God in all things and in serving him by them. Nothing can then really come as an interference between God and his creature, because everything on the contrary becomes a means of encounter and of union. This was what Paul experienced when he exclaimed: "Who shall separate us from the love of Christ? Shall tribulation, or distress, or persecution, or famine, or nakedness, or peril, or sword? . . . For I am sure that neither death nor life, nor angels, nor principalities, nor things present, nor things to come . . . nor anything else in all creation, will be able to separate us from the love of God in Christ Jesus our Lord" (Rom. 8:35, 38, 39).

A magnificent text of Michel Quoist in *Prayers of Life*[1] expresses what I wanted to say in explaining this contemplative attitude as an experience to be practiced:

> If only we knew how to look at life as God sees it, we should perceive that nothing in the world is profane, but that everything contributes to the building of the Kingdom of God. To have faith is not only to raise one's eyes to God

---

1   Michel Quoist, *Prayers of Life* (Dublin, 1963).

to contemplate him; it is also to look at this world—but with Christ's eyes. If we had allowed Christ to penetrate our whole being, if we had sufficiently made our gaze single, the world would no longer be an obstacle. It would be a perpetual incentive to work for the Father in order that, in Christ, his Kingdom might come on earth as it is in heaven.

D. Suggestions for Readings

Teilhard de Chardin: *The Divine Milieu* (New York, 1960), and *Hymn to the Universe* (New York, 1965).

On the experience during the Exercises of the immanence of God following on that of his transcendence, see the conclusion of *Biblical Theology and the Spiritual Exercises*, ch. 8, pp. 312-332. Some other commentaries on the Contemplation to Attain Love are:

H. Urs von Balthasar, "Love—a Wilderness," ch. 13 in *Heart of the World*, pp. 204-219.

J. Laplace, "The Contemplation to Obtain Love," in *An Experience of Life*, pp. 183-187

Ledrus, Meditation 57: "Chercher Dieu en toutes choses."

D. Stanley, *Modern Scriptural Approach*, ch. 32 (pp. 315-324), "Contemplation for Obtaining Love" (with reference to Deut. 26:5-9 and Rom. 8:18-29).

Finally, A. Cannizzo, "La contemplatio ad amorem e gli Esercizi," in *Corso*, lessons 40 and 41, and L. Romano, "Agape ed Esercizi Spirituali."

Chapter 12

APPLYING ONE'S PERSONAL EXPERIENCE
IN A COMMUNITARIAN WAY

Although this topic, spiritual experience in a communitarian way, could be treated in itself and would require a whole book, I shall deal with it here along the same lines as the treatment of "Life in the Spirit" above in chapter 10. One of the ways of prolonging the individual's retreat experience is to go over it again within a group. We shall see that this is, at one and the same time, a response to a call or urge which springs from our faith experience: that desire to live out one's Christian commitment in the company of others, to deepen it, to take up its challenges, to give it every chance of full development within an atmosphere of active "catholicity."

A. The Foundation for This Repetition of the Experience and Occasions for Putting It into Practice

After studying at length the personal spiritual experience, it is not at all contradictory to consider this same experience on a group level and to speak explicitly of its repetition in a communitarian manner. The justification for this lies in the fact of the universal and universalizing character of the content in an individual's experience in Christian faith. In fact, we have seen that the "objective pole" of this personal experience is universal in itself; it embraces God, his creation, and humankind's place in it as it advances toward its goal, the God who made it all. It draws everything into a unity, as we saw when we studied the unifying vision of Christian faith in chapter 3 above. This means that, although the experience is personal, it opens up expansive dimensions of this universal, living reality. Moreover, this faith vision is directly nourished by this inspiring view, so that it encourages one to take one's own part in this advancing history of salvation with more truth and fidelity. To discuss this same experience in a group is directly to actualize this social, universal dimension of the Christian faith experience.

Consequently, we can say that the communitarian spiritual experience will repeat and apply the same directive principles of the experience of Christian faith, by adapting them to a particular mode of evolution. Hence, there will be the same dialectical give and take, the same basic nourishment, the same general procedure (through stages), but on a scale of amplification in proportion to the size of the group.

In the group experience, the relation of the objective to the subjective poles will be the same. We shall survey, on the objective level, the same content as in the retreat experience, God's unfolding plan of creation, salvation, and glorification—St Paul's "mystery of Christ," the marvel of life in Christ our Savior. On the subjective level, the participants in the group will review the same experiences they had in the retreat, but those experiences will be amplified from many points of view. In a group we should learn how to nourish ourselves from the living mysteries of faith; in the same way our assimilation of them can be verified, so that we go forward step by step (in spite of the slower pace and some other difficulties which may perhaps multiply in proportion to the number of persons involved). Here it is a question of a group experience, one lived out in a group; and its development is linked with the presence, commitment, and evolution of each of its members.

From this connection with the principal objective and subjective characteristics of the faith experience, it is fairly evident that our communitarian repetition of the personal spiritual experience lies along the line of the experience of "communities of faith," those "basic communities" (*communautés de base*). In the past few decades they have been springing up in considerable numbers and responding to the desire of many Christians to live in the company of others, where they share their faith experience, their questionings, their hopes and commitments. However, the rather summary analysis I am presenting here does not extend to the phenomenon in its entirety. I am limiting it deliberately to a more intensive period of deepening of experience in a group, just as I did in directing an individual retreatant during the space of a year or more. The other modes of group experience—regular communities of life, work, or reflection— may follow the same method for their communal development; but here I am not considering them directly.

Finally, for my purpose, I shall base my remarks on the experiences which I and some of my colleagues have had during the last few years and which we have discussed together in order to come to some practical conclusions. In fact, these experiences were concerned only with a definite time spent in the group—about a year in most cases—during which our procedure was guided by this method which we had used in directing

"Spiritual Exercises made in everyday life." The meetings were carried on with very different groups: university students from different faculties, students of a major seminary, laymen and laywomen working in various areas, religious living in small communities, Jesuits in their tertianship, an entire family of father, mother, and six children, women who had already been holding regular spiritual meetings, and finally some groups of married couples who were also accustomed to periodic meetings for spiritual sharing.

B. The Chief Conditions for Realizing This Practice

While making use of the same elements used for the personal spiritual experience of the retreat, we must learn how to adapt them to the group and to its way of progressing. So it is necessary to study ways and means of proceeding which will ensure this adaptation to the new conditions of the group experience without breaking away from the inspiration which guided the experiences in the personally directed retreat. If we are accustomed to accompanying individuals, adapting the framework and the means from one person to another, we shall realize that the same holds true when we go from individuals to a group and from one group to another. What, therefore, will be the chief conditions necessary for a spiritual communitarian experience to be valid and successful?

1. Shared Motivations from Basic Communities

On the level of personal experience we have insisted on the basic motivations which make this experience possible: the existence, quality, and maturity of the desire which each member has for this form of commitment. I place these motivations of the base or group as the prime necessity for the group experience. But in this case they must be held in common, that is, shared as such. If at the outset the group is not motivated by a common desire, known and shared, there would be risk of velleities, of superficial efforts and enthusiasms according to prevailing tastes and fashions. On the contrary, a common desire, matured and expressed by the members of the group, involves each one; and, above all, it provides a basic communion of aspirations necessary for a forward spring toward a common goal. Hence, during the time of preparation for the experience itself, there must be an explicit understanding about what urges us to attempt the experience (our motivations) and about what the members are putting into it and expect to get from it (our desires).

2. Some Human Prerequisites

The period of preparation for the retreat experience of an individual gave much importance to the personal history of the retreatant, not only that the director might get to know the retreatant but also to enable the retreatant to catch hold of his or her own history in order to discover how to utilize that past by incorporating it faithfully into the coming faith experience.

This requirement has its clear equivalent on the level of the group. This is true not only for groups which are formed around the experience about to be undergone, and which consist of people who know one another more or less well. In fact, a first nucleus of friends has often been joined by others who were known to be interested, and thus all grow into a group sharing a new experience. But practice has taught us that nearly always, even among people who have known each other for a long time, this requisite remains fully valid. At the point of departure, a mutual acquaintance among the members of the group is not sufficient; they must go further than this and discover behind the familiar features the singular and exciting history of a life which has never stopped progressing.

When the preparation is judged adequate and the members of the group have the true and unanimous desire to go forward, the first stage of knowing one another better can be undertaken, so that their selves, ideas, aims, and the like may be shared, deepened, listened to, and accepted in kindness.

It is fairly important that, when possible, the group help a person to pick out from his or her chronological history, both psychological and sociological, also his spiritual history: his history of faith, his own salvation history, the history of God in his life. For it is on this more lively basic awareness that the spiritual experience of the members and of the group will develop. It will truly be a continuation of a past which opens possibilities for a more deliberate, more energetic, more involved living in the present and the future. This is similar to what had to be done for the personal retreat experience. But in this case the openness and the sharing are amplified, and so are the possibilities for acceptance, kindness, sharing, and discernment. These are, indeed, the fruits which we have drawn from this experience in nearly all the cases we have analyzed.

3. Planning a Spiritual Itinerary

Our team learned from experience that it is important to know how to draw up a definite plan right at the beginning. With the individual who undertakes to make the Exercises in daily life, such a plan was already at hand, fully made. We saw that it is good to take account of it in order to commit oneself, with a more fervent desire and a more dynamic knowledge, along a way open to any adaptation necessary. The same holds true for a group.

Since we are treating of an intensive experience, accompanied or supervised, the director is the one who ought to animate the group to adapt for itself the plan it will follow, in accordance with its own requirements and preferences. Groups already sensitive to spiritual things might be ready to put the plan directly into execution and begin immediately the itinerary suggested by the Exercises; others would need to fashion one from the beginning by using their ingenuity.

Since the liturgy, to which we shall come back later, will in all probability constitute the most natural occasion for the community experience in its more intense moments, it would be an advantage, when possible, to take it as the direct inspiration for drawing up the plan of the group development. In this case the plan could be punctuated by the great liturgical feasts, which would be prepared for by the community on the group level—especially Christmas, Easter, and Pentecost. Sometimes other events concerning the group and its progress could be used as highlights; in certain cases these were an important family anniversary, preparation for a marriage or First Communion, participation in a significant social event.

If this is done, the experience will be undertaken in a more conscious way, will be better shared and accepted by the group from the beginning; while avoiding improvisation as far as possible, it will in no way exclude flexibility and creativity.

4. Some Directives for Communitarian Progress

A first rule, essential for growth either communitarian or individual, and one that is more difficult to discern in the case of a group, is that pertaining to the pace of the experience, a respect for time and its action. To the extent that there is to be a true group experience (I shall come back to this point), the time necessary for each person involved in the experience must be respected. This will mean that the process will require more patience. Without matching exclusively the pace of the slowest, it will always take into consideration each person's pace, impose patience on the faster ones, and urge forward in a respectful way those who are more hesitant. Such compromise, always enriching, is characteristic of a group experience. It also presupposes that each member intends to participate as fully as possible and in all sincerity.

If any excess should enter this practice of respecting each person's pace, I would prefer that it be on the side of waiting for others rather than forcing undue haste in the experience at the expense of some members. Having said this, I might add that if some member's slowness was such as to hinder the advancement and progress of all, one should have the courage in charity to lay the cards on the table so that the experience does not deteriorate under pretext of an exaggerated or misplaced respect. Respect does not immobilize.

A second rule, a consequence of the first, concerns the attention the animator should pay to individuals in the group. It sometimes happens that the group would be spared delays and marking time if the animator could personally intervene and help certain members to become better inserted into the group, to acquire a better personal understanding of the process going on, and to collaborate more effectively in the communitarian movement. Moreover, in addition to this question of overcoming any possible obstacles, the director should, through his or her private contacts with the participants, see to it that each stage has been satisfactorily accomplished as it comes along. A group verification by itself may be insufficient because of factors which involve personal problems in the depths of each one's heart. Insofar as this intervention is possible, desired, and accepted, it should give rise to a second form of accompaniment on the part of the animator or director, who continues to be present to the group as such and to accompany it.

Along the same line as the preceding requirements, we might indicate as another rule the dynamic of an experience in common which can become more and more significant and influential on the progress of the group. In fact, as the experience develops, becomes more personalized, and takes on consistency, this interior dynamism finds expression in initiatives which arise from the experience itself and which can influence and sometimes modify the direction taken at first. We have seen that such was the case for the personal spiritual experience, especially during the Second Week of the Exercises.

A fourth and equally important rule concerns the common understanding to be fostered during the experience. Already at the outset there was a double consciousness awakened in the group—that of the shared motivations which united the members and that of the renewal and deepening knowledge of one another.

To the extent that other common awarenesses will show up, the group will experience beneficial ups and downs and will constantly be renewed. The material of these awarenesses may vary according to whether they arise during the sessions of evaluation of the actual ongoing experience (the subjective level), on the occasion of collective assimilations of particular matters which nourish the experience (the objective level; namely, communion in the same vision of faith, in a shared encounter with the Lord), or even at precise moments of discernment which concern one or other participant but which are realized with the cooperation of the group.

Finally, a last rule, common to every experience which involves communication, is the reminder about the necessity of a language suitable for speaking of realities to be experienced and for fostering dialogue on the group level. Here we are considering the problem of the language of faith, whether there is question of the objective realities of the faith which ought to be encountered in the experience, or of the personal expression of one's own faith experience. In this matter we need great ingenuity, especially on the level of the group, in order to reach every point of view and, on the other hand, to express the interiority and depth of the experiences concerned. To this end, one should not hesitate to have the group seek its own ways of expression: through word, gesture, art, prayer, play, celebration, or the like.

5. Some Means of Proceeding

Continuing the foregoing considerations, I now come to various means which the group may use in the living of its communitarian experience. The ideal will always be for the group to decide for itself, insofar as possible, the means best suited to its own tastes and aptitudes and, progressively, to the dynamism of its own experience.

In practice, certain means are normally used. But what is important here is that each group make use of them as suited to itself—whether it be in regard to meetings, dialogue, prayer (silent, spontaneous, or recited), liturgy, Gospel sharing, revision of life, or anything else. In order to find the best means, the group will proceed with experiences, through trial and error, to decide the frequency of meetings, manner of dialogue and prayer, and its own initiatives.[1]

---

1 The experience of communal spiritual discernment may be situated in this context of the means of expression of a group spiritual experience. While communal discernment is based on personal spiritual discernment, it employs methods or techniques which characterize the discernment made as a group through alternating periods of prayer, dialogue, and analysis of the motions from the Holy Spirit on the group. On it see Jules Toner, "A Method for Communal Discernment of God's Will," *Studies in the Spirituality of Jesuits*, III, no. 4 (September 1971).

6. The Contribution from the Liturgy

In most cases the liturgical cycle has played an important part in community spiritual experience. In fact, the liturgy is the life of the Church, the participation of the whole Church in God's plan of salvation unfolding in the history of salvation. This communion corresponds to an official and constant call on the part of the Church which recapitulates, in time, the whole mystery of Christ and allows us to communicate with it as a group, in a communitarian way.

When the accompaniment of an experience is foreseen for the space of a year, corresponding most frequently to the limits of the academic year, it is easy to divide the stages of progression by following the liturgical cycle rather closely. In this way the weeks or months preceding the time of Advent might be used to ensure the preparatory stages of a serious spiritual experience. This can take the form of a more explicit statement of common motivations, a better mutual acquaintance of the participants, a setting in motion of the experience through a progressive opening to the dimensions of faith in our life (the Principle and Foundation of the Exercises). The stage of formulation of the fundamental vision and of the integration of the problem of evil into this vision of faith and hope (a continuation of the Principle and Foundation plus the First Week of the Exercises) can be arranged to correspond to the four weeks of Advent. With Christmas begins the following of Christ, but in conformity with the dynamic of divine revelation, which the liturgical cycle itself follows. With the beginning of Lent the group will carry out more deeply its personalized progress of conversion, election, and ascent towards the paschal mystery. The time after Pentecost brings us to the period of the nascent Church and of the mission to be lived in the Spirit.

Within this context of the liturgy, certain group experiences have found the means of weekly nourishment and expression with quite a deep appreciation of the road traveled by individuals as well as by the group as such.

C. Different Types of Experience

In speaking of the opportunities for carrying out this group experience, I said above that, in practice, various groups had already tried this method of spiritual animation. The different types of experience which were noticed were the result of the very great variety of the groups. It could also arise from some kinds of commitment. By way of conclusion, I would like to distinguish these in order to aid groups to find their own place among them and profit more from the possibilities open to each group.

I shall reduce these various possibilities to two categories; and within them the variety will come pretty much from the persons involved with their previous experiences, and from the composition of the groups (more homogeneous or more heterogeneous), and the like. These categories might be termed sharing groups and experience groups.

1. The Sharing Group

It is a fact that some people will recognize in one another common desires for spiritual assistance.[2] These will be able to follow a plan of animation based on that of the *Exercises*, with the same content of experience and the same methods of procedure. The whole difference between this group and what I call an experience group lies in the former group's being composed of persons who live their *personal* spiritual experience more intensely within the spiritual group itself and with the help of the spiritual group to which they belong. Instead of being accompanied by one animator or director, as I have taken for granted throughout this book, they go through the same experience, but within a group whose members pursue the same work individually. The originality of this procedure lies in the fraternal sharing of personal experiences. Without doubt the group will also pass through spiritual periods, spiritual experiences at given moments; but the objective envisaged is the progress of the individuals aided by the initiative and the conduct of the experience in the group.

It is evident that the speed of the advance which prevails in this case is that of each individual in his or her own development; the group is merely the occasion for sharing in order to encourage, nourish, and foster the experience of each member. When the communion with the experience with one another has been deepened, it can happen that, at the end, the group may be ready for a real group spiritual experience. But in the meantime, since a group experience is not the primary objective, the criteria by which the analysis of the experience is made cannot be drawn from this undertaking. We remain on the level of individuals, although they are within a group for sharing and support.

2 Many examples of such groups are found in the modern charismatic movement.

2. The Experience Group

An "experience group" is one in which all the members have had a common spiritual experience and now undertake to proceed precisely as a group. This presupposes a certain preexistence and maturity of its group life. Everything that was stated above in this chapter applies also to these "experience groups" of members ready to advance together as a group.

However, this is a matter of application, and the applications may be somewhat different. For although in both groups the activities are carried out in the group, in the sharing group the prime objective is the benefit of the individual member, while in the experience group the chief focus is the benefit of the group as group.

3. Conclusion: A Religious Group

In conclusion I should like to state that the members of a religious community seem to me, by vocation, called to live its communitarian spiritual life on this level. They constitute an experience group rather than one of simple sharing; and they live on a level of religious experience which is not limited to an intense period lived in depth, but which has become the normal expression of life in the Spirit, to which they should bear witness before people in the Church. I have developed this point of view at greater length in a chapter of a book, *Community Spiritual Leadership*.[3] This chapter was written in collaboration with and published by the Canadian Religious Conference. I think that community renewal, especially on the level of small communities, is slowly but surely tending towards this ideal of commitment. In any case, it is the best opportunity we have to attain it. For this reason it should be promoted enthusiastically along this line, and it will then become the inspiration for the many faith communities which are growing up. For persons do not journey alone on the road to eternity to which they are called by the experience of faith and life in the Spirit.

D. Concluding Remarks

Are not the Exercises made in everyday life merely a simple, more intensive, and more organized "spiritual direction" quite distinct from the real, complete Exercises of Thirty Days as presented in St. Ignatius' booklet? This is a question which I am often asked.

My reply is that these Exercises are especially "the Exercises" through

---

3 The chapter entitled "Fraternal Life in the Spirit," pp. 83-96 in *Community Spiritual Leadership*, no. 18, in the series Donum Dei (Ottawa: Canadian Religious Conference, 1971).

the quality of the experience they enable one to live. They follow a dynamic movement which guides the person of the retreatant in an energizing faith towards a progressively committed love. The heart of this experience is always the intimate election which surrenders the person to the experience of conformity with Christ and which qualifies him or her for a total, liberating communion with the paschal mystery of the Lord and of the Church.

It may be well to recall that Ignatius pursued the one same end through both of these methods, one of which he described in the nineteenth annotation and the other in the twentieth. He was confident that the only things to be changed were the circumstances and the setting of the experience.

The experiences I have had in this field during the past years have, however, convinced me in a practical rather than a theoretical way of the complementarity of these two methods. The "open" Exercises made in daily life teach the spiritual experience of Christian faith in actual life situations; through them the exercitant learns how to insert himself or herself immediately into the reality of ordinary living with all that it requires, and how to make it closely related to the vision of faith and the action of the Holy Spirit. The "closed" Exercises of thirty days, on their part, intensify enormously the transforming experience of the immediate encounter with God through a more extended, deepened, undistracted, and fruitful prayer.

All this takes place in a very general way; that is, it excludes what is personal to each retreatant (which remains the most decisive factor). I think I can say that the Exercises in daily life are the most efficacious preparation possible for the Exercises of thirty days, conceived and made according to the spirit of St. Ignatius, and in a context of evangelical radicality which has lasting effects for the person who undertakes it.

But in both the one case and the other, it is essential that the predominant element be the sole good of the believer who undertakes this experience of faith and who offers himself or herself to this action of the Lord. His ways are subtle and hard to define, but his end is always the same: light and life.

> For once you were darkness, but now you are light in the Lord; walk as children of light (for the fruit of light is found in all that is good and right and true), and try to learn what is pleasing to the Lord. Take no part in the unfruitful works of darkness, but instead expose them. For it is a shame even to speak of the things that they do in secret; but when anything is exposed by the light it becomes visible, for anything that becomes visible is light. Therefore it is said, "Awake, O sleeper, and arise from the dead, and Christ shall give you light" (Eph. 5:8-14).

REFERENCE MATTER

Bibliography
Detailed Table of Contents

BIBLIOGRAPHY

Balthasar, H. U. von. *Heart of the World*. San Francisco: Ignatius Press, 1979.

Coathalem, Hervé. Trans. C. J. McCarthy. *Ignatian Insights: A Guide to the Complete Spiritual Exercises*. 2nd ed. Taichung, Taiwan: Kuangchi Press, 1971.

IV Corso internazionale per direttori. Rome: Ignatian Center of Spirituality, 1972.

Cowan, Marian, and J. C. Futrell. "The Nineteenth Annotation Retreat" in *The Spiritual Exercises of St. Ignatius: A Handbook for Directors*. New York: Human Development, 1981

Cusson, Gilles. *Biblical Theology and the Spiritual Exercises: A Method toward a Personal Experience of God as Accomplishing within Us His Plan of Salvation*. St. Louis: The Institute of Jesuit Sources, 1988.

————*Les Exercices dans la vie cotidienne: Résultats d'une enquête (1966-1967)*. Rome: Ignatian Center of Spirituality, 1976.

Evdokimov, P. *L'art d' l'icône: Théologie de la Beauté*. Paris, 1970.

Fitzmyer, J. A. "The Spiritual Exercises and Recent Gospel Study." *Woodstock Letters*, 91 (1962), 246-274.

Fleming, D. L. *The Spiritual Exercises of St. Ignatius: A Literal Translation and a Contemporary Reading*. St. Louis: The Institute of Jesuit Sources, 1978 and 1989.

Giuliani, Maurice. "The Exercises in Daily Life" in *Progresssio*, Supplement No. 19 (November 1981). Rome: Christian Life Communities, Borgo S. Spirito, 15, 00193 Rome, Italy.

Ignatius of Loyola, St. *The Constitutions of the Society of Jesus*. Trans. G. E. Ganss. St. Louis: The Institute of Jesuit Sources, 1970.

Iparraguirre, I. *Práctica de los Ejercicios de San Ignacio de Loyola en vida de su autor (1522-1556)*. Rome: Historical Institute of the Society of Jesus, 1946.

————*Historia de los Ejercicios de San Ignacio. Vol. II (1556-1599)*. Rome: Historical Institute of the Society of Jesus, 1955.

Jacob, Edmond. *Le Dieu Vivant, Foi Vivante*. Paris: Seuil, 1971.

The Jerome Biblical Commentary. Ed. R. E. Brown, J. A. Fitzmyer, R. E. Murphy. Englewood Cliffs: Prentice Hall, 1968. See the index, e.g., s.v. "Biblical Theology," "*Mysterion* (mystery)," "Plan of God," and the like.

Laplace, Jean. *An Experience of Life in the Spirit*. Chicago: Franciscan Herald Press, 1977.

Ledrus, M. *Thèmes pour les Exercices spirituels*. Rome: Ignatian Center of Spirituality, 1973.

Léon-Dufour, Xavier. *Dictionary of Biblical Theology*. New York: Crossroads, 1973.

McCool, F. J. "The Preacher and the Historical Witness of the Gospels." *Theological Studies*, 21 (1960), 517-543.

McKenzie, John L. *Dictionary of the Bible*. New York: Macmillan, 1965 and 1973.

Ricoeur, P. *Fallible Man: Philosophy of the Will*. Chicago: H. Regnery Co., 1967.

Stanley, David M., *Christ's Resurrection in Pauline Soteriology*. Rome: Biblical Institute, 1961. See especially pp. 2-4, The Concept of Biblical Theology, and pp. 232-23, Paul's Personal Experience of Christian Salvation (1 Tim 1:15-16).

————"*I Encountered God!" The Spiritual Exercises with the Gospel of St John*. St. Louis: The Institute of Jesuit Sources, 1986. See especially pp. 311-327, A Suggested Approach to *Lectio Divina*.

————*A Modern Scriptural Approach to the Spiritual Exercises*. St. Louis: The Institute of Jesuit Sources, 1986; also, Chicago: Loyola University Press, 1986. (First printing was in 1967.)

Sullivan, Mary, and D. Horstman. "The Nineteenth Annotation Retreat: The Retreat of the Future." *Review for Religious*, 36 (1972), 277-285.

Teilhard de Chardin, Pierre. *How I Believe*. New York: Harper and Row, 1969.

————*Hymn of the Universe*. New York: Harper and Row, 1965.

Toner, J. J. *A Commentary on St. Ignatius' Rules for the Discernment of Spirits: A Guide to the Principles and Practice*. St. Louis: The Institute of Jesuit Sources, 1982.

Van Schoote, J. P. "Los Ejercicios de San Ignacio según la anotación 19." Ch. 14 in *Los Ejercicios de San Ignacio a la luz del Vaticano II*. Madrid: BAC, 1968.

Veltri, J. *Orientations, Volume II: Annotation 19*. Guelph, Ontario: Loyola Retreat House, 1981.

DETAILED TABLE OF CONTENTS

Table of Contents in Summarized Form   v
Editor's Foreword   vii
Author's Introduction   xi
The Text of the Nineteenth Annotation   2
Abbreviations Used in the Footnotes   2

PART I. GENERAL INTRODUCTON

Ch. 1. The History of "Nineteenth Annotation" Retreats   3

  A. In St. Ignatius' Own Practice (1521-1556)   4
  B. In the Era of the First Generations of Jesuits (1521-1599)   6
    1. The General Practice   7
    2. Some Points in Detail   8
      a. The Selection of Truly Apt Retreatants   8
      b. The Contents of an "Open" Retreat   9
      c. The Prayer   9
      d. The Problem of an Election   9
      e. Visits to the Retreatants   10
      f. The Giving of Notes to the Retreatant   11
    3. The History of These Retreats in Later Centuries   12
    4. Renewal of the Practice in Our Times   13

Ch. 2. The Method in General   17

  A. Some Practical Details   17
  B. The Candidates for the Exercises Made in Everyday Life   18
    1. Their Selection   18
    2. The Requirements   18
    3. The Remote Preparation of the Candidates   20
    4. The Proximate Preparation   21
      a. Its Sequence   21
      b. Its Content   21
      c. An Understanding of the Experience   22
      d. An Overall View of the Coming Retreat   22
        i. With Emphasis on the Objective Level   23
        ii. With Emphasis on the Subjective Level   23
      Fig. 1. St. Ignatius' Divisions of the Exercises   24
    5. A Road to Be Traveled in Six Stages   27
      Fig. 2. Our Journey and Its Six Stages   28

Detailed Table of Contents

PART II: THE EXPERIENCE OF RETREATANTS AND ITS EVOLUTION

Ch. 3. The Viewpoint of Faith Which Puts All Things into a Unified Order: the Principle and Foundation 31

A. The Objective in This First Stage 31
B. Guiding the Retreatant's Experience 32
  1. On the Objective Level of the Message Communicated 33
    a. Presenting the Worldview Which Arises from Our Christian Faith 33
  2. On the Subjective Level of the Retreatant's Experience 36
    a. Explaining the Procedure to Be Used 36
    b. Evaluating the Experience 37
  3. Some Practical Observations 37
    a. The Foundation and the Viewpoint of Faith 37
    b. The Retreatant's Personal Faith History 38
    c. The Comprehensive Character of the Foundation 39
    d. The Ultimate Criterion for the Verification 39

Ch. 4. The First Week: Integrating the Problem of Evil into the Viewpoint of Faith 41

A. The Objective in This Second Stage 41
  1. Relation between the Foundation and the First Week 41
  2. The Problematic and Its Interpretation 43
    a. The Statement of the Problem 44
    b. The Search for an Interpretation 45
    c. The Origin of Evil in the Interpretation of Christian Faith 45
    d. Our Rising above Evil 48
  3. Our Weakness Balanced by Christian Hope 49
B. A Way to the Experience Sought in the First Week 50
  1. The Global History of Evil 50
  2. One's Personal History of Evil 52
  3. The Repetitions 52
  4. Hell 53
C. Some Practical Observations 54
  1. The Transition from the First Principle and Foundation to the First Week 54
  2. The Dynamic Character of the First Week 56
  3. The Place of Christ in the First Week 56
  4. The Result of the First Week 57
  5. Confession 58

Ch. 5. The Second Week: The Kingdom and the Deepening of One's Spiritual Life 59

A. The Place and Objective of the Meditation on the Kingdom 59
  1. The Connection with Ignatius' Worldview 59
  2. In the Context of One's Own Life 60

3. The Precise Objective of This Meditation — 61
B. The Structure of the Ignatian Meditation — 62
  1. A Double Principle of Discernment — 62
  2. The Distribution of the Material — 62
C. The Content of This Exercise in Practice — 63
  1. The Mission of Christ — 63
  2. Our Participation in Christ's Mission — 64
  3. The Oblation: Total and Radical — 65
  4. The Ignatian Parable — 66
D. The Exercitant's Task — 67

Ch. 6. *Christ and His Saving Mission: His Infancy and Hidden Life as a Prelude* — 69

A. Introduction to Section II of the Retreat Experience: Assimilation — 69
  1. A Change of Key — 69
  2. The Three Stages of This Experience — 71
B. A Basic Problem in the Contemplation of the Gospel Mysteries in the Second Week — 72
  1. The Purpose of the Gospel Events in God's Revelation, in the Experience of Living the Spiritual Life, and in the Second Week — 72
  2. A Problem of Exegesis and Contemplation — 72
C. The Infancy and Hidden Life in the Second Week — 73
  1. The Purpose of the Narratives in Matthew 1-2 and Luke 1-2 — 74
  2. The Purpose on the Objective and Subjective Levels during the Second Week — 74
D. The Selection and Distribution of the Subject Matter — 75
  1. The Introductory Contemplation on the Incarnation — 75
  2. Matthew 1-2 and Luke 1-2 — 76
    a. The Hidden Life — 77
    b. Suggested Readings — 79

Ch. 7. *Initiation into Personal Discernment: The "Ignatian Day"* — 81

A. The Place and Meaning of These Meditations in the Second Week — 82
  1. Verification of One's Dispositions — 82
  2. Introduction to the Content or Subject Matter of the Election — 83
B. The Subject Matter of This Introductory Day — 84
  1. The Two Standards — 84
  2. The Three Classes of Persons — 87
  3. The Three Degrees of Humility — 88
C. Some Practical Observations — 90
  1. Attachment to Self—the Devil's First Deceit — 90
  2. The Dispositions Chiefly for This Period in the Retreat Experience — 90
  3. The Language Used — 91
  4. The Possibility of Prolonging These Meditations — 92

5. Some Suggestions on Prayer — 92

Ch. 8. The Public Life: Contemplation on Gospel Events and Simultaneous Deliberations about an Election — 95

A. The Meaning of This Stage — 95
  1. The Sociological and Spiritual Significance of the Public Life — 96
  2. The Function of the Mysteries of the Public Life in Divine Revelation and in the Christian Experience — 97
  3. The Contemplations and the Simultaneous Deliberations for an Election — 98
B. The Contemplations on the Gospel Mysteries: The Hearing of the Word and Acceptance of It — 99
  1. The First Principle on the Objective Level for the Selection of the Gospel Mysteries: The Internal Logic in Christ's Proclamation of His Kingdom — 99
  2. The Second Principle on the Objective Level for the Selection of the Gospel Mysteries: The Four Approaches of the Evangelists in Composing Their Respective Gospels — 101
  3. Another Principle for Selection, on the Subjective Level: The Internal Dynamism of the Retreatant's Spiritual Experience — 101
  4. Practical Conclusions — 102
C. The Work of the Election: Submission to the Action of the Holy Spirit — 102
  1. The Amount of Time to Be Given to the Election — 103
  2. Levels of the Election — 103
  3. Conditions for Realizing the Election — 104
D. Transition from the End of the Election to the Third Week — 105

Ch. 9. The Third and Fourth Weeks: An Experience of Sharing in the Paschal Mystery — 107

A. The Experiential Character of This Stage — 108
  1. The Dynamic Purpose of the Paschal Mystery in Divine Revelation — 108
  2. The All-Embracing Nature of the Paschal Mystery — 109
  3. Our Consent to the Paschal Mystery — 110
  4. Résumé — 111
B. Overall Interpretation of the Chief Events of the Paschal Mystery — 111
  1. The Supper: the Mystery of Salvation in Its Totality — 112
  2. The Reading of the Passion according to the Two Chief Gospel Traditions — 113
  3. The Agony: Awareness of the Sin of the World and Acceptance of Its Guilt — 114
  4. The Trial: the World Judges and Condemns God — 115
  5. The Death of Christ and the Scriptures — 116

6. The Resurrection: The New Life Offered to Creation and to
    Humankind   116
7. The Apparitions: Appropriation of the Fruit of the Resurrection   117
8. The Ascension: Return to the Universal—Spirit and Mission   119
C. The Spiritual Fruits of This Stage   119
D. Suggestions for Readings on the Third and Fourth Weeks   121

PART III. PROLONGATIONS OF THE EXPERIENCE OF THE EXERCISES

Ch. 10. Life in the Spirit after the Exercises Have Ended   125

A. The Exercises as an Apprenticeship to Life in the Spirit   125
B. The Regime of the Holy Spirit   127
C. Some Requirements for Life in the Spirit   128
    1. Charity   128
    2. Prayer   129
    3. Obedience   130
    4. Spiritual Discernment   131

Ch. 11. Prolongations of the Retreat Experience in a Personalized
    Manner   135

A. The Simple Repetition of the Experience   135
B. The Circularity of the Experience   136
C. The Contemplation to Increase Our Love for God   137
D. Suggestions for Readings   140

Ch. 12. Applying One's Personal Experience in a Communitarian Way 141

A. The Foundation for This Repetition of the Experience and
    Occasions for Putting It into Practice   141
B. The Chief Conditions for Realizing This Practice   143
    1. Shared Motivations from Basic Communities   143
    2. Some Human Prerequisites   144
    3. Planning a Spiritual Itinerary   144
    4. Some Directives for Communitarian Progress   145
    5. Some Means of Proceeding   147
    6. The Contribution from the Liturgy   147
C. Different Types of Experience   148
    1. The Sharing Group   149
    2. The Experience Group   150
    3. Conclusion: A Religious Group   150
D. Concluding Remarks   150

REFERENCE MATTER

Bibliography   155